The fight against
in the imperialist

CW00543825

The fight against Jew-hatred and pogroms in the imperialist epoch

Stakes for the international working class

V.I. LENIN
LEON TROTSKY
FARRELL DOBBS
JAMES P. CANNON
JACK BARNES
DAVE PRINCE

Pathfinder

NEW YORK   LONDON   MONTREAL   SYDNEY

Edited by Dave Prince, Steve Clark, Mary-Alice Waters

ISBN 978-1-60488-172-1
Library of Congress Control Number: 2024935482
Manufactured in Canada

First edition, 2024

COVER DESIGN: Toni Gorton

COVER PHOTOS:

LEFT: Poland, 1943: After crushing month-long uprising by Jews in Warsaw Ghetto, Nazi storm troopers round up Jewish women, children, and men for death camps. (United States Holocaust Museum)

RIGHT: Gaza Strip, October 7, 2023: Hamas thug grabs hold of Naama Levy, 19, one of 240 hostages seized that day in southern Israel. Some 1,200 people were murdered and thousands wounded in the Hamas-led pogrom.

PATHFINDER
www.pathfinderpress.com
Email: pathfinder@pathfinderpress.com

CONTENTS

ABOUT THE AUTHORS

II

CHAPTER 1
The fight against Jew-hatred
and pogroms in our epoch

19

CHAPTER 2
Lenin and the Bolsheviks: A united workers party
and the fight against pogroms

43

CHAPTER 3
Proletarian internationalism,
not reactionary bourgeois nationalism

59

CHAPTER 4
Continuing Lenin's course in face of
Stalinist counterrevolution

69

CHAPTER 5
Forging a proletarian party in the United States:
The 1930s and World War II

85

CHAPTER 6
The Socialist Workers Party in the fight
against Jew-hatred and pogroms today

115

APPENDIX

129

Hamas in its own words
Hamas's fascist roots lie in Hitler's 'Final Solution'

SOURCE NOTES

143

GLOSSARY

147

EXPANDED CONTENTS

ABOUT THE AUTHORS   11

CHAPTER 1
**The fight against Jew-hatred
and pogroms in our epoch**   19

Dave Prince

CHAPTER 2
**Lenin and the Bolsheviks: A united workers party
and the fight against pogroms**   43

Jews aren't workers' enemies; the enemies are
   the capitalists everywhere (V.I. Lenin, March 1919)   44

Pogroms are fatal to the workers and peasants
   revolution (V.I. Lenin, July 1918)   45

Massacres of Jews rouse disgust of working people
   around the world (V.I. Lenin, January 1917)   47

Organize self-defense against pogroms
   (V.I. Lenin, June 1906)   49

What is a pogrom? (V.I. Lenin, December 1911)   51

No nationality in Russia is so oppressed and
   persecuted as the Jews (V.I. Lenin, March 1914)   52

A great international revolution (Leon Trotsky, 1929)   54

A centralized proletarian party strengthens the force
   of our offensive (V.I. Lenin, February 1903)   55

Forging a larger American movement
   (James P. Cannon)   57

CHAPTER 3
**Proletarian internationalism,
not reactionary bourgeois nationalism**   59

Communists back movements to help educate and
   organize exploited toilers (V.I. Lenin, July 1920)   60

CHAPTER 3 (*continued*)

To advance national liberation, combat reactionary
forces in the colonial world (V.I. Lenin, June 1920)   61

The Jewish question can't be solved in the
framework of capitalism (Leon Trotsky, 1934)   66

CHAPTER 4
**Continuing Lenin's course in face of
Stalinist counterrevolution**   69

'I declare war on Great Russian chauvinism'
(V.I. Lenin, October 1922)   70

Lenin's letter on the national question to the
Twelfth Party Congress (L. Fotieva, April 1923)   71

'Not the slightest crudity or injustice toward
other nationalities' (V.I. Lenin, December 1922)   72

The program of international revolution
or socialism in one country (Leon Trotsky, 1928)   73

The Stalinist regime is reviving the anti-Semitic
tradition of tsarism (Leon Trotsky, January 1937)   77

Setbacks to revolution breed unbridled chauvinism
and Jew-hatred (Leon Trotsky, February 1937)   82

The struggle against imperialism and war
(Leon Trotsky, September 1938)   84

CHAPTER 5
**Forging a proletarian party in the United States:
The 1930s and World War II**   85

Workers self-defense, not reliance
on the bosses' state (Farrell Dobbs)   87

Our course on Jewish question: The international
class struggle (SWP Political Committee, 1938)   100

Open doors to refugees from Hitler's Nazi terror!
(SWP National Committee, November 1938)   102

CHAPTER 5 (*continued*)

Protect workers meetings and Jews menaced by
fascists (James P. Cannon, November 1941)   104

The task is to create a defense guard in unions
(Leon Trotsky talks with SWP leaders, 1938)   110

The fight against fascism begins in the factory
and ends in the street (Leon Trotsky, 1938)   111

CHAPTER 6
**The Socialist Workers Party in the fight
against Jew-hatred and pogroms today**   115

To end Jew-hatred, fight to win workers power
and socialism (Rachele Fruit, October 10, 2023)   116

Workers power: The indispensable political weapon
to combat all oppression (Jack Barnes)   118

A party whose integrity, conduct match
its working-class aims (SWP, 2022)   122

APPENDIX   129
Hamas in its own words:
Jew-hatred, genocide, anticommunism   129

Hamas's fascist roots lie in Hitler's 'Final Solution'
(Terry Evans)   135

SOURCE NOTES   143

GLOSSARY   147

PHOTOS AND ILLUSTRATIONS

SWP presidential candidate condemns Hamas
pogrom, 2023 / 1917 Russian Revolution 21

Hamas parades body of Israeli, 2023 /
Hamas and Tehran leaders meet, 2024 25

US bombardment during Gulf War, 1991 /
Ukrainians resist Moscow's invasion, 2022 27

Hamas apologists: New Orleans, 2023;
Berkeley, 2024 30

Lenin records speech against pogroms, 1919 /
Red Army liberates Odessa, 1919 33

Post-World War II "displaced persons" camp /
London attacks and turns back Exodus, 1947 38

Trotsky and Red Army during civil war, 1918 /
Belostok pogrom, 1906 48

Anti-imperialist revolts in China and Egypt, 1919 62

Lenin speaks to Communist International, 1920 /
Pogrom in British-ruled Palestine, 1929 63

Nazi storm troopers, 1933 / Spanish Revolution and
sit-down strikes by French workers, 1936 76

Stalin wields Jew-hatred against Trotsky /
Moscow Trials, 1937 / "Doctors' Plot," 1953 79

Teamsters make Minneapolis a union town, 1934 /
Union Defense Guard routs fascists, 1938 98

Pickets say: "Let Jewish refugees in!" 1938 /
50,000 take on pro-Nazi rally, New York, 1939 99

Minneapolis frame-up trial and World War II, 1941 /
Flint auto workers' sit-down strike, 1937 106

SWP candidate at march against Jew-hatred,
2024 / Auto workers' strike gains, 2023 117

Montgomery bus boycott, 1955 / Malcolm X
in Selma, 1965 / Leo Frank lynching, 1915 120

Fidel Castro: "This is our socialist revolution!" 1961 /
  Cuban combatants in Angola, 1988   124
Hamas leader: "We'll do this again!" October 2023 /
  Tehran: "Drive Jews into sea!", 2023   138
Amin al-Husseini meets with Hitler, 1941, and reviews
  Waffen SS troops in Bosnia, 1943   139

V.I. LENIN

V.I. Lenin (1870–1924) was the central leader of the Bolshevik Party, which led workers and peasants to power in the world's first socialist revolution in October 1917. He was chairman of the revolutionary government in the Union of Soviet Socialist Republics (USSR) from its founding in 1922 until his death.
Lenin was the founding leader of the Communist International, which worked to advance the building of proletarian parties worldwide, parties able to emulate what toilers in Russia had accomplished in conquering state power.

Before taking state power, the Bolshevik Party, under Lenin's leadership, stood in the front ranks of those fighting pogroms organized by the hated tsarist regime. After the October victory they acted decisively on their program guaranteeing all oppressed nationalities, including the Jews, the right to self-determination. The Bolshevik Party led the revolutionary government and Red Army to defeat the counterrevolutionary armies organized by the imperialist powers. They carried out their pledge to use all means necessary, including mobilization of the Red Army, to defend Jewish settlements against the pogromist Cossack and other counterrevolutionary armies and "tear the anti-Semitic movement out by the roots."

In the final year of his active political life, Lenin led the fight within the Communist Party of the Soviet Union against the counterrevolutionary political course of the growing petty-bourgeois and newly emerging bourgeois layers in the Soviet Union that Joseph Stalin came to represent.

LEON TROTSKY

Leon Trotsky (1879–1940) was part of the central leadership forged by Bolshevik Party leader V.I. Lenin that organized the revolutionary conquest of power by workers and peasants in Russia in October 1917.

Following the revolutionary victory, among other leadership responsibilities, Trotsky commanded the Red Army, which defeated counterrevolutionary troops, routed invading forces from sixteen countries, and defended Jews against counterrevolutionary-led pogroms during the 1918–1920 Civil War.

Trotsky was one of the founding leaders of the Communist International in 1919. Following Lenin's death in 1924, he led the communists in the Soviet Union and worldwide who fought to continue Lenin's proletarian internationalist course. He continued that struggle from exile after being deported in 1929 by the anti-Leninist majority in the government of the USSR headed by Joseph Stalin.

In 1938, working together with the leadership of the Socialist Workers Party in the US, Trotsky drafted the program of the world movement he led. Known as the Transitional Program, it was adopted that year by the founding conference of the Fourth International.

The fight against all forms of chauvinism, "particularly anti-Semitism, should become part of the daily work" of all sections of that movement, he wrote. "Our basic slogan remains: Workers of the World Unite!"

In 1940 Trotsky was assassinated in Mexico by Stalin's secret police.

FARRELL DOBBS

Farrell Dobbs (1909–1983), national secretary of the Socialist Workers Party from 1953 to 1972, emerged from the ranks of the Teamsters as a central leader of battles that transformed the union movement during the Great Depression.

Dobbs was a leader of the 1934 strikes that made Minneapolis a union town and of the organizing drives that brought a quarter million over-the-road truck drivers into the Teamsters union across the Midwest and Mid-South.

In the late 1930s, as groups supporting fascism began to emerge across the country, Minneapolis Teamsters set a national example in organizing a workers defense guard. The unit—made up of 600 volunteers from unions in the area, trained and drilled by military veterans—successfully defended union headquarters and Jewish organizations from attack by fascist thugs.

During World War II, Dobbs and other class-struggle leaders propagandizing for a labor party and organizing working-class opposition to Washington's war aims were railroaded to federal prison by the US imperialist rulers. Dobbs resigned as general organizer on the Teamster national staff in 1940 to become labor secretary of the Socialist Workers Party. He was the party's presidential candidate four times.

JAMES P. CANNON

James P. Cannon (1890–1974) was born in Rosedale, Kansas, and joined the Socialist Party at the age of eighteen. A traveling organizer for the Industrial Workers of the World before and during World War I and a leader of the working-class left wing of the Socialist Party, he was a founding leader of the communist movement in the United States, which was organizing to emulate what the workers and peasants of Russia had achieved.

Cannon spent seven months in Soviet Russia from June 1922 to January 1923, where he was a delegate to the Fourth Congress of the Communist International held in Moscow and a member of the presidium of the Executive Committee of the Communist International.

He later served as executive secretary of the International Labor Defense in the United States, a nationwide organization that fought for the release of any class-war prisoner framed up for militancy in the workers movement regardless of political affiliation.

Together with a number of other veteran leaders of the Communist Party, Cannon was expelled in 1928 for supporting Leon Trotsky's political fight to continue the revolutionary internationalist course of V.I. Lenin.

Cannon was a founding leader in 1929 of the Communist League of America, which became the Socialist Workers Party in 1938. He served as SWP national secretary until 1953, then national chairman until 1972.

JACK BARNES

Jack Barnes is national secretary of the Socialist Workers Party. He joined the SWP in May 1961 and has been a member of the party's National Committee since 1963 and a national officer since 1969.

Barnes joined the Young Socialist Alliance in December 1960, soon after a trip to revolutionary Cuba in July and August that year. On his return, he helped organize at Carleton College in Minnesota one of the largest and most active campus chapters of the Fair Play for Cuba Committee. He has been a leader of the party's defense of Cuba's socialist revolution ever since.

While organizer of the SWP branch in Chicago and YSA Midwest organizer in the early 1960's, Barnes was a central leader of the successful four-year campaign to defend three YSA members in Bloomington, Indiana, indicted in

1963 for "assembling" to advocate the overthrow of the State of Indiana by force and violence.

In 1965 he was elected YSA national chairman and became director of the SWP and YSA's work to advance the growing movement against the Vietnam War. In January 1965 Barnes met twice with Malcolm X to conduct an interview published in the *Young Socialist* magazine a few weeks after Malcolm's assassination, the last interview Malcolm was to give and approve before its publication.

Since the mid-1970s Barnes has led the political course of the SWP and its sister parties worldwide to build communist parties whose members and leaders in their large majority are workers and unionists organizing workers to forge and strengthen trade unions and lead the working class and its allies toward a successful socialist revolution.

DAVE PRINCE

Dave Prince, a member of the National Committee of the Socialist Workers Party since 1977, was drawn into working-class political activity in the early 1960s while a student at Oberlin College in Ohio and then Tyler Art School in Philadelphia. The mass Black working-class struggle that brought down the Jim Crow system of institutionalized racial segregation had a powerful impact on his political course. He was an early partisan of Cuba's socialist revolution, defender of Malcolm X, and builder of what became millions-strong actions demanding the US government "Bring the Troops Home Now!" from Vietnam.

Prince joined the Young Socialist Alliance and Socialist Workers Party in fall 1965 in Cleveland, Ohio. Over the years he has taken on a broad variety of central leadership responsibilities. He helped lead the party's industrial trade union fractions in the International Union of Electrical Workers (IUE) and United Auto Workers (UAW), as well as in unorganized machinists and meatpacking shops.

During the 1990s and early 2000s, Prince headed the party's print shop in New York, which produced the *Militant* newsweekly and books published by Pathfinder Press.

Today, among other responsibilities, Prince leads the work with the party's worldwide network of organized supporters.

CHAPTER 1

The fight against Jew-hatred and pogroms in our epoch

DAVE PRINCE

The Fight Against Jew-Hatred and Pogroms in the Imperialist Epoch: Stakes for the International Working Class is published as hundreds of millions are being drawn into world politics by the unfolding crisis of the imperialist system and its ramifications in every corner of the globe. The rise in Jew-hatred and violence that has marked the opening decades of the twenty-first century—from the Middle East to North and South America, Europe, Africa, Asia, and the Pacific—is deeply rooted in this global crisis.

Jew-hatred is a *world* question. The fight against it is decisive to every working-class battle today against the brutal consequences for humanity of imperialism and its convulsions.

This book presents the political foundations and continuity of the Marxist program and course—in history and in action—on these questions. Jew-hatred is not eternal; it is rooted in class-divided society and the class struggle. And the authors answer the all-important question: *What is to be done to end it*—for all time.

The pages that follow include excerpts from articles and speeches by V.I. Lenin, the central builder of the Bolshevik Party and leader of the October 1917 Russian Revolution. Lenin addresses the decisive place of the battle against Jew-hatred and pogroms in the fight for the socialist revolution necessary to overturn the tsarist empire. Under Lenin's leadership, the Bolshevik Party placed itself on the front lines of that battle, from its formation in 1902–03 to Lenin's death in 1924.

The battle against persecution of Jews was intertwined with the fight for the right of all oppressed nations to self-determination. It was intertwined with the fight against reactionary bourgeois nationalism and chauvinism—in the young Soviet republic and in other lands where revolutionary struggles inspired by the victorious October 1917 revolution exploded.

The book includes Leon Trotsky's international fight in the 1920s and 1930s to defend Lenin's communist continuity against the political counterrevolution in the Soviet Union and Communist Party led by Joseph Stalin. The articles and interviews by Trotsky excerpted here were written during the years when mounting Jew-hatred and anti-Semitic violence were harbingers of what was to be the second inter-imperialist world war and the Holocaust.

There are writings by central leaders of the Socialist Workers Party from its founding onward—James P. Cannon, Farrell Dobbs, and Jack Barnes—presenting the course of action that guides the SWP to this day.

Imperialism and Jew-hatred

The persecution of Jews goes back two millennia.

But with the dawn of the imperialist epoch in the final years of the nineteenth century, the weight and place of Jew-hatred in social relations changed. It became an *inter-*

In the fight against Jew-hatred, the Socialist Workers Party is part of the continuity going back to Lenin and the Bolsheviks.

MARY MARTIN/MILITANT

LEFT: Rachele Fruit, Socialist Workers Party candidate for US president, speaks to press at October 10, 2023 event at Miami's Holocaust Memorial to condemn Hamas pogrom in Israel three days earlier. "The fight to end Jew-hatred will take a working-class struggle for power, a socialist revolution," she said.

RIGHT: Working people demonstrate in Petrograd during 1917 Russian Revolution. The Bolshevik Party under Lenin's leadership led workers to take state power in October 1917 and overturn capitalist rule. It set an example of the kind of working-class leadership that needs to be forged today—a communist leadership, tested in struggle, confident in the revolutionary capacities of the working class.

national question, an expression of the intense virulence of the capitalist economic and social convulsions that erupted in the imperialist First and Second World Wars.

The "international Jewish conspiracy" became the common banner of fascist movements. Under that banner, they sought to justify attacks on the working class and its political vanguard, as well as other toilers, and to smash their unions and parties. The triumph of fascism across much of Europe, intertwined with the advancing Stalinist political counterrevolution in the USSR, guaranteed the conflagration to come. Over these decades there was a sharp rise of pogroms—the brutal slaughter of Jews—and then the intensified assault with Adolph Hitler's "Final Solution," the mass extermination of six million Jews, in the final years of the war.

So long as the dictatorship of capital remains—based on class exploitation and capitalist control of production and exchange—there is no solution to imperialism's recurring march toward fascism and war. Modern capitalism's international domination, and the fight among the main imperialist powers and their ruling families to partition the world, makes recurring social crises and wars inevitable. And it also makes inevitable resistance and revolutionary upsurges by the working class and all the exploited.

The Jewish question itself is a class question.

As we are seeing again today, Jew-hatred has a permanent place and function for the propertied ruling families in the imperialist epoch.

The way forward for the international working class is through building revolutionary proletarian parties, commu-

---

For terms, places, and individuals, see glossary at end of book.

nist parties, in the countries where we live. Revolutionary leaderships that have unshakeable confidence in the working class and oppressed to take their destiny in their own hands. To organize along the working-class line of march toward engaging the propertied ruling classes worldwide, taking state power, and transforming society.

The October 7 pogrom

The October 7, 2023 slaughter of Jews in Israel carried out by Hamas's squads of murderers and rapists was a pogrom, reactionary to the core.

It was made possible by the advance planning and full financial and logistical support from the counterrevolutionary capitalist regime in Iran. Tehran and its top government and clerical leaders publicly celebrated the massacre, which also involved several smaller Jew-hating groups, primarily Islamic Jihad and the Popular Front for the Liberation of Palestine.

The new stage of the war against Jews and the State of Israel launched by Hamas that day still rages as this book is published. In addition to the battles being fought in Gaza, attacks on civilian populations in Israel have been launched from Lebanon by Hezbollah, Hamas's Tehran-spawned ally. There are ongoing terrorist operations by groups tied to the Iranian regime operating in Yemen, Iraq, and Syria.

These events mark a watershed in the worldwide imperialist crisis, with unknowable consequences. They are part of the profound shift already registered by the first large-scale land war between two state powers in Europe since World War II, opened by the February 2022 invasion of Ukraine by Vladimir Putin's Great Russian chauvinist regime. Moscow's aim is to drown in blood the Ukrainian people's independence and sovereignty, their existence as a nation.

Contrary to the claim by the Hamas organizers, and by supporters and cheerleaders of the October 7 pogrom, that mass slaughter of Jews was not an anti-imperialist action in any sense. It had nothing to do with advancing the interests of the Palestinian people, or of the exploited and oppressed anywhere in the world.

October 7 was not a military operation in a national liberation war. To the contrary. The pogrom was organized and carried out by trained death squads—thugs, murderers, rapists—indiscriminately slaughtering, maiming, torturing, and sexually abusing individual *Jews,* regardless of nationality, age, or sex.

The victims were Jewish men, women, children, and infants from kibbutzim near the border between Israel and Gaza, as well as those attending a large international music festival. The death squads murdered some 1,200 people, wounded more than 5,000, and took hostage more than 240.

Jewish women were raped and then murdered, often gang raped, sometimes in front of family members to further degrade and humiliate them. Women's bodies were mutilated and desecrated. Hostages have been, and are being, subjected to further torture and abuse.

Hamas also killed, brutalized, or took hostage several dozen migrant workers from Thailand, the Philippines, Sri Lanka, and elsewhere, as well as a number of Israeli Arabs. That was not a mistake by Hamas. These workers were considered a legitimate target of the pogrom simply because they had associated with Jews.

This was a pogrom like those instigated against Jews by the tsarist regime in Russia in the late nineteenth and early twentieth centuries. The Russian monarchy's only answer "to demonstrations of the people demanding free-

The October 7, 2023, slaughter of Jews in Israel carried out by Hamas death squads was a pogrom, reactionary to the core.

ABED ABU REASH/AP

WEST ASIA NEWS AGENCY

TOP: October 7, 2023. Body of Jewish man murdered by Hamas death squads in Israel is paraded through streets of Gaza City. Contrary to claims by Hamas and its cheerleaders, the mass slaughter of Jews had nothing to do with the interests of the Palestinian people, or the exploited and oppressed anywhere in the world.

BOTTOM: Tehran, March 26, 2024. Iran Supreme Leader Ali Khamenei meets with Hamas leader Ismail Haniyeh. Tehran's long-standing support made possible the October 7 massacre. Its top leaders celebrated the pogrom, calling for "the eradication of the cancerous Zionist tumor."

dom," wrote Lenin in 1911, "is to let loose gangs of men who seize hold of Jewish children by their legs and smash their heads against stones, who rape Jewish and Georgian women and rip open the bellies of old men."

Nothing had changed on October 7 from the Bolshevik leader's description more than a century earlier.

The October 7 slaughter was the worst single act of violence against Jews since the Holocaust carried out by the Nazis. It has irrevocably shaken hopes and illusions of Jews and others that escalating acts of Jew-hatred are a historical aberration, a thing of the past. That they are exceptions to the rule. That they will die down. Or that Washington and other "democratic" imperialist governments can be counted on to defend Jews at home or anywhere in the world.

What does the future have in store? Is Jew-hatred eternal?

The global order imposed by the victors of the imperialist slaughter of World War II has been breaking down. For decades US imperialism, the earth's final empire, has been weakening. But the US rulers' existence is based on two interlinked goals. One is their ceaseless rivalry to dominate all their imperialist competitors. The other, vital to capitalism's survival, is to crush the development of revolutionary struggles by the toilers anywhere in the world. That includes Washington's multifaceted, "never forgive and never forget" efforts over decades to punish Cuban working people for their audacity in making Cuba's socialist revolution.

Washington's 1991 war against Iraq—ending with the US Command's infamous "turkey shoot" of tens of thousands of retreating Iraqi troops and civilians—sounded the opening guns of World War III. That prospect is not an

The global order imposed by the victors of World War II has been breaking down, with explosive ramifications for working people everywhere.

RIGHT: Road from Kuwait to Basra, Iraq, where US bombing slaughtered thousands of retreating Iraqi soldiers and civilians, February 1991. That war, which accelerated rivalry between Washington and other imperialist powers, sounded the opening guns of World War III. Today that prospect is an unfolding reality.

ABOVE: Kherson, Ukraine, March 2022. Residents chanting "Go home!" resist Russian military invasion and occupation, aimed at crushing Ukrainian people's existence as a nation. After eight months of brutal occupation, Ukrainian forces liberated Kherson.

The October 7 pogrom in Israel and the Putin regime's invasion of Ukraine—the first major land war in Europe since World War II—mark a watershed in the worldwide imperialist crisis.

anticipation; it's an unfolding reality. Only the pace and how it will unfold are still to be resolved. Only the working class, through victorious revolutionary action, can take the power and wrench the ability to make war out of the hands of the propertied rulers.

There have been two such great proletarian revolutions in the past century. The first was the October Revolution in Russia led by Lenin and the Bolshevik Party he forged. The other was Cuba's socialist revolution led by Fidel Castro and the cadres of the Rebel Army and July 26 Movement he commanded.

Each of these revolutions set an example of the political character of proletarian leadership that can and must be forged—communist leadership, tested in struggle, and acting with confidence in the revolutionary capacities of the working class and the oppressed.

Fascist roots of Hamas

Hamas, founded in 1987, has its roots both in the landed classes and monarchies in the Arab world of the 1920s and 1930s, and in anti-working-class bourgeois nationalist currents and parties across the region ever since.

These ruling classes stood in opposition to revolutionary developments among working people in Palestine and elsewhere in the Middle East, developments that were inspired by the example of the Russian Revolution and were welcomed by its Bolshevik leadership. Communist parties, which initially drew together revolutionary-minded workers of Jewish, Arab, and other national origins, were formed in Palestine, Egypt, and elsewhere in the Middle East.

In the 1930s and 1940s, the Egypt-based Muslim Brotherhood and related reactionary currents forged direct relationships with fascists in Italy and especially Adolph Hitler's Nazi party in Germany.

Trotsky's description of the culture of fascism in a May 1940 manifesto, "The Imperialist War and the Proletarian World Revolution," is accurate, more than eight decades later, as to how Hamas and its backers function today. "The sole feature of fascism that is not counterfeit is its will to power, subjugation, and plunder," Trotsky wrote. "Fascism is a chemically pure distillation of the culture of imperialism."

Tehran, Hezbollah, Hamas, and their supporters proclaim to the world their commitment to more pogroms. Their banner is Jew-hatred: another Holocaust, completing the unfinished "Final Solution." They reject any "solution" other than the physical elimination of Jews, not just in the Middle East but the world over. Seven million of the earth's 15.7 million Jews today live in Israel, and a similar number in the United States, with smaller but significant numbers in other countries.

Jew-hatred is the banner under which the bourgeois-clerical regime in Iran justifies its expansionist drive—often carried out by terrorist groups that Tehran arms and funds in neighboring countries—to extend the regime's counterrevolutionary military and economic domination across the Middle East. Tehran's declared aim of getting rid of the Jews and eliminating Israel is made even more dangerous for toilers everywhere by its accelerated course toward developing and deploying a strategic nuclear arsenal.

The Palestinian people have paid an enormous price for this genocidal Jew-hating course of "From the river to the sea, Palestine will be free." Their lives and futures are sacrificed by Hamas leaders, who organize their operations centers and artillery installations inside, nearby, or under-

"From the river to the sea, Palestine will be free" is Hamas's genocidal goal: Drive out the Jews! Kill the Jews!

Apologists for Hamas demonstrate at Tulane University in New Orleans, October 27, 2023.

Berkeley, February 26, 2024. Pro-Hamas thugs at University of California stormed building where Jewish student groups had invited Israeli army reservist to speak at a meeting. They banged on and smashed windows, forcing evacuation of audience. Some who call themselves "socialists" and champion Hamas will find themselves allied with future fascist forces.

neath hospitals, schools, and apartment buildings in Gaza. They use civilians as human shields. They educate children to aspire to "martyrdom," not to life. They organize and act with the collusion of United Nations agencies and personnel. In order to meet Hamas's own needs, its armed thugs seize relief supplies, including food and medicine, intended for the Palestinian people.

The greatest danger to Jews and all the oppressed in the region and worldwide is the call for a ceasefire *before* Hamas has been defeated and its leadership and command structures demolished. Far from being a "pacifist" response to war, the international propaganda clamor for a ceasefire had been planned by Hamas and its cohorts' years before October 7, 2023. *It's a Hamas campaign.*

And the Democratic Party administration of Joseph Biden—confirming once again the anti-working-class foundations of the US imperialist government—is bringing to bear it weight against Israel's right to defend itself as a refuge for Jews, demanding that it declare a ceasefire before the command structures of Hamas have been destroyed.

Only the unequivocal defeat of Hamas, however, can open up space for Jewish, Arab, and other working people to find a way forward, together, in revolutionary struggles against the capitalist rulers of Israel, Palestine, and elsewhere in the region.

Forging a revolutionary proletarian party

Lenin's course in combating the persecution of Jews was part of forging the proletarian program, organizational norms, and habits of conduct of the Bolshevik Party.

That course guided the party's actions before, during, and after the October 1917 revolution in Russia, both in the young workers state itself and through the Communist International founded at the Bolsheviks' initiative in 1919 to build proletarian parties dedicated to extending the world socialist revolution.

The tsarist empire's ousted capitalist factory owners and landowners organized a murderous three-year-long civil war to reclaim their property and power, with decisive assistance from the invading armies of London, Paris, Berlin, Washington, and other imperialist governments.

As part of the battles that crushed the counterrevolution, the Red Army—initiated and led by Lenin, and under the command of Leon Trotsky—fought and defeated the pogromists. Those victorious battles inspired Jews and other toilers not only in the former tsarist empire but around the world.

"The tsarist police, in alliance with the landowners and the capitalists, organized pogroms against the Jews," explained Lenin in a 1919 speech reproduced on a phonograph recording that was widely distributed across the Soviet republic.

"The landlords and capitalists tried to divert against the Jews the hatred of workers and peasants who were tortured by want. In other countries too, we often see the capitalists fomenting hatred against the Jews in order to blind the workers, to turn away their attention from the enemy of working people, capital," the Bolshevik leader said.

"Shame on accursed tsarism which tortured and persecuted the Jews. Shame on those who foment hatred towards the Jews, who foment hatred toward other nations. Long live the fraternal trust and fighting alliance of the workers of all nations in the struggle to overthrow capital."

The Bolsheviks championed the rights of all oppressed nationalities in the former tsarist empire, including the millions of Jews.

TOP: "It's not the Jews who are the enemies of working people—it's the capitalists of all countries," said V.I. Lenin in a 1919 speech. The talk was widely circulated on a phonograph record by the revolutionary government brought to power in October 1917.

CENTER: The day the Bolshevik-led revolutionary government took power, it issued a statement, addressed "To Workers, Soldiers, and Peasants," guaranteeing "all nations within Russia the genuine right to self-determination."

BOTTOM: Odessa, Ukraine, 1919. Crowds greet Red Army soldiers who liberated the city—which had the largest Jewish population in tsarist Russia—from counterrevolutionary forces. By the end of the civil war in 1921, Red Army had put an end to anti-Jewish pogroms. Its ranks, as the photo shows, included working people of many nationalities.

The Socialist Workers Party "is part of the continuity in the fight against Jew-hatred that goes back to Lenin and the Bolshevik Revolution in Russia," declared the SWP in its very first statement on Hamas's October 7 pogrom. That statement—issued by Rachele Fruit at a protest of the slaughter held at Miami's Holocaust memorial—is reprinted in this book. Fruit is currently the SWP's 2024 candidate for president of the United States.

This Bolshevik continuity was carried forward by Trotsky in the fight in the late 1920s and 1930s to maintain Lenin's proletarian internationalist course against the bloody political counterrevolution led by Joseph Stalin. In materials in this book, Trotsky describes how the Stalinist bureaucracy fostered anti-Semitism in the Soviet Union, targeting those defending Lenin's program and actions. Many of them, including Trotsky, were Jewish. Anti-Semitism was used against those targeted by Stalin's notorious Moscow frame-up trials and executions between 1936 and 1938, during which virtually the entire remaining central leadership of the October Revolution was killed.

The SWP in those years—working closely with Trotsky, then living in exile in Mexico—took on the struggle against the devastating social consequences for working people of the deep worldwide capitalist depression and social crisis and the march toward a second imperialist war. Trotsky warned of rising fascist movements among the panicked petty bourgeoisie and middle classes, driven by their fear of the abyss, accompanied by "a monstrous growth of violent anti-Semitism in all the world."

At the close of the 1930s, as the US rulers prepared to enter the spreading world war in defense of their own capitalist interests, communist workers in the SWP fought and won a political battle against a minority faction in the party who were caving to the pressures of escalating war propaganda and the social milieu of the rulers' middle-class mouthpieces. The opposition broke from Marxism over the inseparable questions of opposing US imperialist war aims and deepening the party's proletarian composition and orientation to the working class and unions.

The SWP's successful struggle for a proletarian party was decisive to its response to efforts among the propertied ruling families to unleash fascist thugs and scapegoat Jews for capitalism's mounting ills. They sought to divert the anger of the insecure or ruined middle classes and layers of working people away from the capitalist rulers responsible for the unemployment, farm foreclosures, and other consequences of the social and economic crisis of the 1930s.

Included here are accounts by two former national secretaries of the SWP, Farrell Dobbs and James P. Cannon. They describe the broad-based union defense guard organized in Minnesota in 1938 that defeated employer-instigated efforts by a US fascist organization, the Silver Shirts, to break the Teamster union and stop developments toward independent working-class political action. Promoting Jew-hatred was an integral part of the fascists' demagogy, of course. After catching wind of the Silver Shirts' union-busting plans, Minneapolis rabbi Albert Gordon turned to the Teamsters to respond to this rightist danger. A public display of the workers defense guard with broad support in the working class led the fascists to scuttle their plans and get out of town.

Workers and trade unionists in New York subsequently sought collaboration with the Minneapolis Teamsters leaders to resist union busting and Jew-hatred by fascist forces there and in neighboring New Jersey. They mobilized for a demonstration of 50,000 in New York City, initiated by the Socialist Workers Party, that countered a rally of 20,000 by the fascist German-American Bund at Madison Square Garden.

No refuge for Jews in imperialist epoch

"From the river to the sea, Palestine will be free" is nothing new. In the words of Hamas's 1988 founding covenant itself, the Jew-hating premise of that slogan "has been laid out in the *Protocols of the Elders of Zion*," the notorious 1905 forgery by the tsarist secret police allegedly proving "plans for universal domination by international Jewry."

From Hitler's *Mein Kampf* and Nuremburg rallies, to the Hamas Covenant, and today's rationalizations for October 7—it all has the same anti-working-class foundations.

The message is clear: *Drive out the Jews! Kill the Jews!* From the Jordan River to the Mediterranean Sea—and anywhere else on earth Jews can be tracked down and targeted, from a synagogue to a kosher grocery, from a dance festival to a nursery or schoolyard. Destroy Israel as a refuge for the Jews.

In the imperialist epoch, there can be no permanent refuge for the Jews. That can only be changed with the victory of proletarian revolution in decisive parts of the world.

The "river-to-the-sea" campaign has nothing to do with the national aspirations of any oppressed people—in Palestine, Iran, the Middle East, North Africa, or elsewhere. Nothing to do with the fight against imperialism by oppressed and exploited toilers. Nothing to do with the working-class struggle for emancipation from the dictatorship of capital and the exploiting ruling classes.

To the contrary, the international campaign for an immediate ceasefire serves only the class interests of the reactionary bourgeois-nationalist leaderships of the regime in Iran, as well as Hamas, Hezbollah, Islamic Jihad, and a handful of others. And it is used by the world's most powerful, ruthless ruling classes, led by those in the United States, to advance *their* global economic, military, and political interests and class domination.

What is to be done?

The establishment of Israel became inevitable with the Second World War.

In the years leading up to and during World War II, the dominant imperialist powers slammed the doors on all but marginal Jewish immigration. That was the course of Washington and London, led by Franklin Delano Roosevelt and Winston Churchill, and followed by the ruling classes of Canada, Australia, and others.

In the aftermath of the war—after Hitler's genocidal extermination of 40 percent of the world Jewish population, six million human beings—the imperialist victors in Washington and London kept their own borders shut tight for three more years. They pushed more than 250,000 Jewish survivors into barely livable "displacement camps" in the defeated European countries of Germany, Austria, and Italy.

Where were the Jews to go?

Prospects for an extension of the socialist revolution in Europe were betrayed by the Stalinist regime and its national Communist Parties. In the early 1930s they sabotaged revolutionary opportunities that could have united the workers movement in Germany and defeated the Nazis in Germany before their consolidation of power. In

Only with the working-class conquest of power and end of the imperialist world order can another Holocaust be stopped.

WOLF SCHÄRF

THE **MILITANT**

MONDAY, AUGUST 4, 1947

THE MILITANT

PAGE THREE

4,500 Jews Get Another Lesson in "Democracy"

British Seize Refugee Ship

By Evelyn Atwood

For the past 12 days, 1,500 Jewish refugees, among them 1,000 women and children, bound for Palestine, have undergone bloodshed and torture at the hands of the British imperialists that Hitler could hardly excel.

Packed like sardines in an ancient American ferryboat renamed *Exodus 1947,* this mass of tired, hungry, unwashed people, clad in rags, sleeping on boards, endured their hardships in the hope of finding a place where they could begin a new, decent life for themselves and their children.

About 17 miles out of Haifa, six British warships — five destroyers and one cruiser — opened up savage warfare on the little vessel and its defenseless occupants. The warships smashed into the *Exodus* from three directions, enveloping the ship in a cloud of fire bombs, gunfire, tear gas. Huge portions of the ship were reduced to kindling wood.

SCORES WOUNDED

For more than three hours, while women and children screamed, the murderous assault continued. Twenty men fell seriously wounded, five lay dying, a hundred were injured. William Bernstein, 24, of Los An-

stretchers, the Jewish immigrants were ordered aboard three British ships, the **Empire Valour, Ocean Vigour** and **Runnymede Park** for re-shipment to France. Food supplies were far from sufficient for such multitudes.

British officials still claim that the refugees were well treated. The condition of the involuntary passengers revealed quite the contrary. Several died as a result of ill treatment or of wounds. According to a Reuters dispatch, a Jewish doctor who went aboard the **Runnymede Park** said there was an epidemic of diarrhoea among the children. But reports about the condition of the ship's occupants could not be verified, since newspaper men were forbidden even to approach the ships. The wretched people could be observed only through field glasses. Some were peering through portholes. Others were standing on decks which were completely compartmented with barbed wire.

TOP: Post-World War II "displaced persons" camp in Austria. After Hitler's extermination of 40 percent of world Jewish population, Washington and London kept their borders closed and shunted 250,000 Jewish survivors into such camps. Where were Jews supposed to go?

BOTTOM: British forces raid refugee ship *Exodus* in July 1947, denying 4,500 Jews entry to Palestine and forcing them back to Europe. Three Jews on ship were killed, dozens injured.

1936–37 they undermined a prerevolutionary situation in France by joining a so-called Popular Front government in alliance with a wing of the capitalist class. They turned their guns against revolutionary-minded workers fighting the fascist forces in Spain that triumphed over the toilers in 1939. Proletarian victories in one or more of those countries could have stopped the human catastrophe of the Second World War.

After the war, revolutionary struggles in Greece, France and Italy by armed workers, looking to find a road toward socialist revolution, were blocked by Stalinist-led parties, in order not to disrupt the postwar carve-up of "spheres of influence" across Europe by Moscow, Washington, and London. On the ashes of the war, the imperialist Democratic and Republican Parties established a new Washington-dominated world order—one that has now begun to fracture.

Under the mantle of the fight against fascism, the imperialists rationalized their rapacious war aims by portraying the populations of both Germany and Japan as uniformly reactionary. But the fire bombings by the US and British imperialist armed forces of working-class neighborhoods in major German and Japanese cities were aimed at blocking workers' struggles after the war. As was Washington's dropping of atomic bombs on both Hiroshima and Nagasaki.

It was this history, these class-struggle realities, that made the establishment of Israel inevitable. Not a "realization of Zionism." Despite efforts by London and Washington to use divide-and-rule policies against Jews and Arabs alike (as the colonizing powers did in India and Pakistan, across Africa, and elsewhere), Israel's existence was not the imposition of a "colonial settler state."

Israel became inevitable as a *refuge* for the Jews. But not a *solution* to Jew-hatred or pogroms. There is no safe haven for Jews in the imperialist epoch, anywhere in the world.

Defense of Israel's right to exist is based on that history. It is a country that offers sanctuary to Jews, anywhere, anytime, in face of persecution and violence.

Only under such conditions will working people in Israel and the region—of Jewish, Palestinian, and other national origins—have the political space to build mutual trust and unity in common struggle. And such class solidarity, in turn, opens the road to forging a communist party, a proletarian party, capable of leading the working class and its oppressed and exploited allies toward a socialist revolution.

Various Zionist currents today wrongly persist in the claim that Jew-hatred is eternal. Some also argue that the persecution of Jews has its roots in inherent prejudices in the working class, permanently necessitating an insular bourgeois Jewish state. But the opposite is true.

In fact, the deepest *abhorrence* of the October 7 pogrom is found in the working class in the United States and elsewhere. It is there—*not* among privileged professionals and the middle classes, or on university campuses, where Jew-hatred is flourishing today—that communist workers find the greatest openness to the fight against the persecution of Jews. It is among working people that communists get a hearing on why the stakes for the labor movement in fighting Jew-hatred and pogroms are so great.

Lenin was right in 1903 when he insisted on "the link that *undoubtedly* exists between anti-Semitism and the interests of the bourgeoisie, and not the interests of the working-class sections of the population."

In 1937 Trotsky posed the question of whether or not a world socialist federation would make it possible "for those Jews who wish to have their own autonomous republic as the arena of their own culture" to do so. A proletarian government would never "resort to compulsory assimilation," he said, and it might "very well be that within two or three generations the boundaries of an independent Jewish republic, as of many other national regions, will be erased...."

"I have in mind a transitional historical period when the Jewish question, as such, is still acute and demands adequate measures from a world federation of workers' states," Trotsky added. An autonomous Jewish republic "under the regime of a socialist federation [would] take on a real and salutary meaning.... How could any Marxist, or even any consistent democrat, object to this?"

In Trotsky's 1938 "Appeal to American Jews Menaced by Fascism," he explained that the most virulent anti-Semitism can be expected in the strongest imperialist powers, "above all in the United States." Amid world capitalism's deepening economic and social catastrophe and fascist advances, Trotsky said, "It is possible to imagine without difficulty what awaits the Jews at the mere outbreak of the future world war. But even without the war the next development of world reaction signifies with certainty the *physical extermination of the Jews*."

"Now more than ever," the Bolshevik leader concluded, "the fate of the Jewish people—not only their political but also their physical fate—is indissolubly linked with the emancipating struggle of the international proletariat."

Those words remain true. A victorious socialist revolution in the United States is both necessary and possible. What's needed, what must be built, is a revolutionary working-class party politically armed with a communist program and a battle-tested proletarian leadership.

That is what the Socialist Workers Party is fighting to build. The party of the American socialist revolution. A revolutionary transformation—part of an expanding *world* socialist revolution—that opens the road to rebuilding society on foundations of human solidarity.

March 30, 2024

Lenin and the Bolsheviks: A united workers party and the fight against the pogroms

From the opening of the twentieth century, V.I. Lenin led the political fight in the tsarist empire's massive "prison house of nations" for a united and centralized working-class party—a party incorporating all those who agreed with its program, regardless of their language, national, or religious origin.

That disciplined revolutionary workers party, known as the Bolsheviks from 1903 on, joined the front lines of the fight against anti-Jewish pogroms promoted by Russia's capitalist rulers. The Bolshevik-led proletarian government brought to power by the victorious October 1917 revolution put a stop to those brutal attacks on Jews.

The young Soviet government was defended by the newly formed volunteer Red Army, led by Lenin and commanded by Leon Trotsky. Its backbone came from the ranks of the most politically conscious workers of all nationalities throughout the former tsarist realm. In a bitter war lasting some three years, they not only crushed the counterrevolutionary armies of Russia's toppled capitalists and landowners. They also defeated the invading armies of imperialist powers from London and Paris, as well as from Washington, Tokyo, and others.

The survival and victory of the new workers state was due in no small part to the intransigent battle the Bolsheviks waged—before, during, and after the October victory—to defend the rights of all oppressed nationalities, including the millions of Jews, across the former tsarist empire. The Bolsheviks educated the toilers about the origins and reactionary character of Jew-hatred. Lenin's two opening pieces from 1918–19 are examples.

Jews aren't working people's enemies, the enemies are capitalists of all countries

FROM SPEECH ON PHONOGRAPH RECORD

V.I. LENIN, MARCH 1919

Anti-Semitism means spreading enmity towards the Jews.[1] When the accursed tsarist monarchy was living its last days it tried to incite ignorant workers and peasants against the Jews. The tsarist police, in alliance with the landowners and the capitalists, organized pogroms against the Jews. The landowners and capitalists tried to divert against the Jews the hatred of the workers and peasants who were tortured by want. In other countries, too, we often see the capitalists fomenting hatred against the Jews in order to blind the workers, to turn away their attention from the enemy of the working people, capital. . . .

It is not the Jews who are the enemies of the working people. The enemies of the workers are the capitalists of all countries. Among the Jews there are working people, and they form the majority. They are our brothers, who, like us, are oppressed by capital; they are our comrades in the struggle for socialism.

Among the Jews there are kulaks, exploiters, and capitalists, just as there are among the Russians, and among people of all nations. The capitalists strive to sow and foment hatred between workers of different faiths, different nations, and different races. Those who do not work are kept in power by the power and strength of capital. Rich Jews, like rich Russians, and the rich in all countries, are in alliance to oppress, crush, rob, and disunite the workers.

Shame on accursed tsarism, which tortured and persecuted the Jews. Shame on those who foment hatred toward the Jews, who foment hatred toward other nations. Long live the fraternal trust and fighting alliance of the workers of all nations in the struggle to overthrow capital.

◆

Pogroms are fatal to the workers and peasants revolution

FROM RESOLUTION OF THE
COUNCIL OF PEOPLE'S COMMISSARS

V.I. LENIN, JULY 1918

According to reports received by the Council of People's Commissars, the counterrevolutionaries are carrying on agitation for pogroms in many cities, especially in the fron-

---

For terms, places, and individuals, see glossary at end of book.

tier zone, as a result of which there have been sporadic outrages against the toiling Jewish population.[2] The bourgeois counterrevolution has taken up the weapon that has slipped from the hands of the tsar.

The absolutist government, each time when the need arose, turned the wrath of the peoples directed at itself against the Jews, at the same time telling the uneducated masses that all their misery comes from the Jews....

In the Russian Socialist Federated Soviet Republic, where the principle of self-determination of the toiling masses of all peoples has been proclaimed, there is no room for national oppression. The Jewish bourgeois are our enemies, not as Jews but as bourgeois. The Jewish worker is our brother.

Any kind of hatred against any nation is inadmissible and shameful.

The Council of People's Commissars declares that the anti-Semitic movement and pogroms against the Jews are fatal to the interests of the workers and peasants revolution and calls upon the toiling people of Socialist Russia to fight this evil with all the means at their disposal.

National hostility weakens the ranks of our revolutionaries, disrupts the united front of the toilers without distinctions of nationality, and helps only our enemies.

The Council of People's Commissars instructs all Soviet deputies to take uncompromising measures to tear the anti-Semitic movement out by the roots. Pogromists and pogrom-agitators are to be placed outside the law.

◆

Massacres of Jews rouse disgust of working people around the world

FROM SPEECH TO SWISS WORKERS
ON THE 1905 RUSSIAN REVOLUTION

V.I. LENIN, JANUARY 1917

Tsarism vented its hatred particularly upon the Jews.[3]

On the one hand, the Jews furnished a particularly high percentage (compared with the total Jewish population) of leaders of the revolutionary movement. And now, too, it should be noted to the credit of the Jews, they furnish a relatively high percentage of internationalists, compared with other nations.

On the other hand, tsarism adroitly exploited the basest anti-Jewish prejudices of the most ignorant strata of the population in order to organize, if not to lead directly, *pogroms*—over 4,000 were killed and more than 10,000 mutilated in 100 towns. These atrocious massacres of peaceful Jews, their wives and children roused disgust throughout the civilized world. I have in mind, of course, the disgust of the truly democratic elements of the civilized world, and these are *exclusively* the socialist workers, the proletarians.

Even in the freest, even in the republican countries of Western Europe, the bourgeoisie manages very well to combine its hypocritical phrases about "Russian atrocities" with

The Bolshevik-led revolutionary government and Red Army stopped the pogroms, inspiring Jews and other working people the world over.

TOP: Leon Trotsky, as commander of Red Army, addresses soldiers, 1918. In civil war, Red Army defeated armies of Russia's former capitalists and landlords backed by invading imperialist force. It put an end to anti-Jewish persecution.

CENTER: Jewish family assaulted in 1906 Belostok pogrom, where reactionary gangs murdered 80 Jews. Since before 1917 revolution, Lenin and Bolsheviks called on workers to organize self-defense militias against anti-Jewish violence.

BOTTOM: Anti-Semitic poster, circulated by counterrevolutionaries in 1919, depicts Red Army commander Leon Trotsky as Jewish "devil."

the most shameless financial transactions, particularly with financial support of tsarism and imperialist exploitation of Russia through export of capital, etc.

Organize self-defense against pogroms

V.I. LENIN, JUNE 1906

Far too much inflammable material has accumulated in Russian social life.[4] The struggle whose way has been paved by ages of unprecedented violence, torment, torture, robbery, and exploitation has become too widespread and acute.... Even the most downtrodden and ignorant "subjects" can no longer be restrained from proclaiming the demands of awakening human and civic dignity. The old authority, which has always made the laws itself, which in fighting for its existence is resorting to the last, most desperate, savage and furious methods, cannot be restrained by appeals to abide by the law.

The pogrom in Belostok is a particularly striking indication that the government has taken to arms against the people. The old but ever new story of Russian pogroms!—ever, until the people achieve victory, until the old authorities are completely swept away....

The police organize the pogrom beforehand. The police instigate it: leaflets are printed in government printing offices calling for a massacre of the Jews. When the pogrom begins, the police remain inactive. The troops quietly look on at the exploits of the Black Hundreds.

But later these very same police go through the farce of prosecuting and trying the pogromists. The investigations and trials conducted by the officials of the old authority always end in the same way: the cases drag on, none of the pogromists are found guilty, sometimes even the battered and mutilated Jews and intellectuals are dragged before the court, months pass—and the old, but ever new story is forgotten, until the next pogrom....

Yes, the downtrodden and tormented Jewish population is indeed apprehensive of [being blamed for their own persecution], and has every reason to be.... This is true. But it is *not the whole truth*, gentlemen, members of the Duma....

You know that the downtrodden inhabitants will *not dare* to name those who are *really responsible* for the pogrom. *You* [the liberal bourgeois and reformist social democratic deputies who claim to oppose tsarism] *must name them*. That is what you are people's deputies for. That is why you enjoy—even under Russian law—*complete* freedom of speech in the Duma. Then don't stand *between* the reaction and the people, at a time when the armed reaction is strangling, massacring, and mutilating unarmed people. Take your stand *openly and entirely* on the side of the people.

Don't confine yourselves to conveying the fear of the townspeople that the vile instigators of the pogroms will say it is the murdered victims who are to blame. *Indict the culprits in unequivocal terms*—it is your direct *duty* to the people. Don't ask the government whether measures are being taken to protect the Jews and to prevent pogroms, but ask how long the government intends to shield the real culprits, who are members of the government. Ask the government whether it thinks that the people will long be in error as to who is really responsible for the pogroms.

Indict the government openly and publicly. Call upon the people to organize a militia and self-defense as the *only* means of protection against pogroms....

[A tsarist deputy in the Duma] bluntly stated that the allegation that pogroms are due to racial enmity was a *lie*, and that the allegation that they were due to the impotence of the authorities was a malicious invention. [He] listed a number of facts that proved that there had been "collaboration" between the police, the pogromists, and the Cossacks. "I live in a big industrial district," he said, "and I know that the pogrom in Lugansk, for example, did not assume ghastly dimensions *only because*—mark this, gentlemen: only because—the *unarmed workers* drove back the pogromists with their bare fists, at the risk of being shot by the police."

◆

What is a pogrom?

V.I. LENIN, DECEMBER 1911

The only answer the Russian monarchy can give to the demonstrations of the people demanding freedom is to let loose gangs of men who seize hold of Jewish children by their legs and smash their heads against stones, who rape Jewish and Georgian women and rip open the bellies of old men.[5]

◆

No nationality in Russia is so oppressed and persecuted as the Jews

FROM THE NATIONAL EQUALITY BILL

V.I. LENIN, MARCH 1914

The Russian Social-Democratic Labor group [Bolsheviks] in the Duma has decided to introduce in the Fourth Duma a bill to abolish the restrictions on the Jews and other non-Russians.[6] The text of this bill you will find below.

The bill aims at abolishing all national restrictions against all nations: Jews, Poles, and so forth. But it deals in particular detail with the restrictions against the Jews. The reason is obvious: no nationality in Russia is so oppressed and persecuted as the Jewish.

Anti-Semitism is striking ever deeper roots among the propertied classes. The Jewish workers are suffering under a double yoke, both as workers and as Jews. During the past few years, the persecution of the Jews has assumed incredible dimensions. It is sufficient to recall the anti-Jewish pogroms....

In view of these circumstances, organized Marxists must devote proper attention to the Jewish question.

It goes without saying that the Jewish question can effectively be solved only together with the fundamental issues confronting Russia today. Obviously, we do not look to the [Great Russian chauvinist] Fourth Duma to abolish the restrictions against the Jews and other non-Russians. But it is the duty of the working class to make its voice heard.

And the voice of the *Russian* workers must be particularly loud in protest against national oppression.

A BILL FOR THE ABOLITION OF ALL RESTRICTIONS ON THE JEWS AND OF ALL RESTRICTIONS ON THE GROUNDS OF ORIGIN OR NATIONALITY

1. Citizens of all nationalities inhabiting Russia are equal before the law.

2. No citizen of Russia, regardless of sex and religion, may be restricted in political or in any other rights on the grounds of origin or nationality.

3. All and any laws, provisional regulations, riders to laws, and so forth, which impose restrictions upon Jews in any sphere of social and political life, are herewith abolished. Article 767, Vol. IX, which states that "Jews are subject to the general laws in all cases *where no special regulations affecting them have been issued*" is herewith repealed. All and any restrictions of the rights of Jews as regards residence and travel, the right to education, the right to state and public employment, electoral rights, military service, the right to purchase and rent real estate in towns, villages, etc., are herewith abolished, and all restrictions of the rights of Jews to engage in the liberal professions, etc., are herewith abolished.

4. To the present law is appended a list of the laws, orders, provisional regulations, etc., that limit the right of the Jews, and which are subject to repeal.

A great international revolution

LEON TROTSKY, 1929

Leon Trotsky, who was chairman of the Petrograd Soviet of Workers and Soldiers Deputies, was second only to Lenin in assuring the victory of the October Revolution that brought the working class to power in Russia. A few days later, Lenin proposed to Trotsky that he head the commissariat (ministry) responsible for state security and the police in the new revolutionary government. The exchange with Lenin was described by Trotsky in his 1929 book My Life.

[Lenin] insisted that I take over the commissariat of the interior, saying that the most important task at the moment was to fight off a counterrevolution.[7]

I objected, and brought up, among other arguments, the question of nationality. Was it worthwhile to put into our enemies' hands such an additional weapon as my Jewish origin?

Lenin almost lost his temper. "We are having a great international revolution. Of what importance are such trifles?"

A centralized proletarian party strengthens the force of our offensive

V.I. LENIN, FEBRUARY 1903

In 1903 two decisive political battles were fought in the Russian Social Democratic Labor Party that established the character of a revolutionary party capable of leading the working class to power. The first came to a head early that year, when a group within the RSDLP called the Bund broke from the party and proclaimed itself an "independent" organization of Jewish workers.

Calling this split "the height of folly," Lenin rejoined that a workers organization capable of overthrowing tsarism and the dictatorship of capital had to be a politically centralized party of cadres from all backgrounds, not a federated party of autonomous national groups.

The second political battle, at the RSDLP's second congress later that year, gave birth to the Lenin-led Bolsheviks—a unified party of all revolutionaries in Russia open to every member who "accepts its program" and "supports the party both financially and by personal participation in one of the party organizations."

Below are excerpts from Lenin's February 1903 article responding to the split by the Jewish Bund.

The Bund has only confused the issue and planted ideas in the minds of Jewish workers that tend to *blunt* their class-consciousness.[8] From the viewpoint of the struggle for political liberty and for socialism by the whole working class of Russia, [the split] is the height of folly....

And this profoundly regrettable fact is not accidental. Having once demanded "federation" instead of autonomy in matters concerning the Jewish proletariat, you were *compelled* to proclaim the Bund an "independent political party" in order to carry out this principle of federation *at all costs*.

However, declaring the Bund an independent political party reduces to an absurdity your fundamental error in the national question, which will inescapably and inevitably be the starting point of a change in the views of the Jewish proletariat and of Jewish Social-Democrats in general.

"Autonomy" under the Rules adopted in 1898 provides the Jewish working-class movement with all it needs: propaganda and agitation in Yiddish, its own literature and congresses, the right to advance separate demands to supplement a single general Social-Democratic program and to satisfy local needs and requirements arising out of the special features of Jewish life.

In everything else there must be complete fusion with the Russian proletariat, in the interests of the struggle waged by the entire proletariat of Russia. As for the fear of being "steamrolled" in the event of such fusion, the very nature of the case makes it groundless, since it is autonomy that is a guarantee against all "steamrolling" in matters pertaining specifically to the *Jewish* movement.

But in matters pertaining to the struggle against the autocracy, the struggle against the bourgeoisie of Russia as a whole, we must act as a single and centralized militant organization. We must have behind us the whole of the proletariat, without distinction of language or nationality, a proletariat whose unity is cemented by the continual joint solution of problems of theory and practice, of tactics and organization.

We must not set up organizations that would march separately, each along its own track. We must not weaken the force of our offensive by breaking up into numerous independent political parties. We must not introduce estrangement and isolation and then have to heal an artificially implanted disease with the aid of these notorious "federation" plasters.

Forging a larger American movement

JAMES P. CANNON

Additional light on Lenin's opposition to fragmentation of a centralized proletarian party along national lines is shed by the following account from The First Ten Years of American Communism: Report by a Participant *by James P. Cannon.*

Cannon was a founding leader of the Communist Party in the United States in 1919. In its first few years, he was part of a political current advocating the CP's transformation from a federated structure of competing immigrant-based language groups into a revolutionary centralist proletarian party, politically organized along Bolshevik lines.

In the brief excerpt below, Cannon recalls the contribution by the party's Jewish members to this fight for the "Americanization" of the CP, as this transformation was referred to in the party at that time.

There was a sound basis for our alliance with the Jewish leaders.[9]

It may seem incongruous that a new fight for "Americanization," with an outspoken proletarian, trade-union,

Midwestern orientation, and a native American leadership, should begin with an alliance with the Jewish leaders, who were all New Yorkers and intellectuals to boot. But it was not as contradictory in life as it looks in cold print.

The Jewish communists were, by far, more assimilated in American life than the other foreign language groups; they had a more realistic appreciation of the decisive significance of a party leadership which would appear to be a genuine American product.

They wanted to be a part of a larger American movement, and not merely the leaders of a futile sect of New Yorkers and foreign-born communists. I think this was their main motivation in allying themselves with us, and it was a politically sound motivation on their part.

CHAPTER 3

Proletarian internationalism, not reactionary bourgeois nationalism

The October 1917 Bolshevik Revolution inspired one of the greatest revolutionary advances in human history, comparable only to the depth and impact of the overthrow of the French monarchy in 1789.

Coming out of the imperialist carnage of World War I, the working class of Germany as well as Hungary strove to emulate the workers and peasants of the tsarist empire. Rising labor battles spread across the United Kingdom, Italy, the United States, and other countries. Rebellions against imperialist domination shook the colonial world across Asia, the Middle East, Africa, and the Americas.

Lenin's report to the Second Congress of the Communist International in 1920 on the "Theses on the National and Colonial Questions," plus his draft of that resolution itself clearly marked out the class lines along which revolutionary workers organizations are obligated to distinguish among political movements and organizations in colonial and semicolonial countries. Always and everywhere, the aim is to advance working-class political consciousness in the struggle against imperialism and to advance the world socialist revolution.

Leon Trotsky's 1934 comments on the fight against the persecution of the Jews question are rooted in the same communist framework, both in theory and in practical consequences.

◆

Communists back movements to help educate and organize exploited toilers

FROM REPORT ON NATIONAL AND COLONIAL
QUESTIONS, SECOND CONGRESS
OF THE COMMUNIST INTERNATIONAL

V.I. LENIN, JULY 1920

It is beyond doubt that any national-revolutionary movement can only be a bourgeois-democratic movement, since the overwhelming mass of the population in the backward countries consist of peasants, who represent bourgeois-capitalist relations.[1] It would be utopian to believe that proletarian parties in these backward countries, if indeed they can emerge in them, can pursue communist tactics and a communist policy, without establishing definite relations with the peasant movement and without giving it effective support.

However, the objection has been raised that, if we speak of the bourgeois-democratic movement, we shall be obliterating all distinctions between the reformist and the revolutionary movements. Yet that distinction has been very clearly revealed of late in the backward and colonial countries, since the imperialist bourgeoisie is doing everything in its power to implant a reformist movement among the oppressed nations too.

There has been a certain rapprochement between the bourgeoisie of the exploiting countries and that of the colonies, so that very often—perhaps even in most cases—the bourgeoisie of the oppressed countries, while it does support the national movement, is in full accord with the imperialist bourgeoisie, that is, joins forces with it against all revolutionary movements and revolutionary classes. This was irrefutably proven in the commission, and we decided that the only correct attitude was to take this distinction into account and, in nearly all cases, substitute the term *national revolutionary* for the term *bourgeois democratic.*

The significance of this change is that we, as Communists, should and will support bourgeois liberation movements in the colonies only when they are genuinely revolutionary, and when their exponents do not hinder our work of educating and organizing in a revolutionary spirit the peasantry and the masses of the exploited.

To advance national liberation, combat reactionary forces in the colonial world

FROM DRAFT THESES ON NATIONAL AND COLONIAL
QUESTIONS, SECOND CONGRESS
OF THE COMMUNIST INTERNATIONAL

V.I. LENIN, JUNE 1920

Petty-bourgeois nationalism proclaims as internationalism the mere recognition of the equality of nations, and noth-

"Communists support bourgeois liberation movements in the colonies only when they are truly revolutionary, when their representatives do not hinder us in educating and organizing the masses of the exploited in a revolutionary spirit."
—V.I. Lenin, 1920

Anti-imperialist revolt in Shanghai, China, June 1919. Example of Russian Revolution encouraged a new rise of anticolonial and revolutionary struggles in Asia and the Mideast.

Egyptian peasants demonstrate in Cairo during uprising against British rule, March 1919.

RIGHT: Lenin speaks at Second Congress of Communist International, July 1920, Petrograd, Russia. The Comintern under Lenin's leadership championed struggles against colonialism and imperialist oppression.

Lenin said communists "need to combat Pan-Islamism and similar trends" that "attempt to strengthen the position of the khans, landowners, mullahs, etc."

ABOVE: Survivors of August 1929 pogrom in British-ruled Palestine, in which more than 130 Jews were massacred. The assault was instigated by reactionary Islamist forces that sought to divert sentiment against British colonialism toward anti-Jewish violence.

ing more.[2] Quite apart from the fact that this recognition is purely verbal, petty-bourgeois nationalism preserves national self-interest intact, whereas proletarian internationalism demands, first, that the interests of the proletarian struggle in any one country should be subordinated to the interests of that struggle on a world-wide scale, and, second, that a nation which is achieving victory over the bourgeoisie should be able and willing to make the greatest national sacrifices for the overthrow of international capital.

Thus, in countries that are already fully capitalist and have workers' parties that really act as the vanguard of the proletariat, the struggle against opportunist and petty-bourgeois pacifist distortions of the concept and policy of internationalism is a primary and cardinal task.

11) With regard to the more backward states and nations, in which feudal or patriarchal and patriarchal-peasant relations predominate, it is particularly important to bear in mind:

First, that all Communist parties must assist the bourgeois-democratic liberation movement in these countries, and that the duty of rendering the most active assistance rests primarily with the workers of the country the backward nation is colonially or financially dependent on.

Second, the need for a struggle against the clergy and other influential reactionary and medieval elements in backward countries.

Third, the need to combat Pan-Islamism and similar trends, which strive to combine the liberation movement against European and American imperialism with an attempt to strengthen the positions of the khans, landowners, mullahs, etc.

Fourth, the need, in backward countries, to give special support to the peasant movement against the landowners, against landed proprietorship, and against all manifestations or survivals of feudalism, and to strive to lend the peasant movement the most revolutionary character by establishing the closest possible alliance between the West-European communist proletariat and the revolutionary peasant movement in the East, in the colonies, and in the backward countries generally. It is particularly necessary to exert every effort to apply the basic principles of the Soviet system in countries where precapitalist relations predominate—by setting up "working people's Soviets," etc.

Fifth, the need for a determined struggle against attempts to give a communist coloring to bourgeois-democratic liberation trends in the backward countries. The Communist International should support bourgeois-democratic national movements in colonial and backward countries only on condition that, in these countries, the elements of future proletarian parties, which will be communist not only in name, are brought together and trained to understand their special tasks, i.e., those of the struggle against the bourgeois-democratic movements within their own nations. The Communist International must enter into a temporary alliance with bourgeois democracy in the colonial and backward countries, but should not merge with it, and should under all circumstances uphold the independence of the proletarian movement even if it is in its most embryonic form.

Sixth, the need constantly to explain and expose among the broadest working masses of all countries, and particularly of the backward countries, the deception systematically practiced by the imperialist powers, which, under the guise of politically independent states, set up states that are wholly dependent upon them economically, financially, and militarily. Under present-day international conditions there is no salvation for dependent and weak nations except in a union of Soviet republics.

◆

The Jewish question can't be solved in the framework of capitalism

FROM INTERVIEW WITH
'CLASS STRUGGLE' MAGAZINE

LEON TROTSKY, FEBRUARY 1934

QUESTION: Does the Left Opposition have to make special demands to win the Jewish working class in America?[3]

LEON TROTSKY: The role of the foreign-born Jewish worker in the American proletarian revolution will be a very great one, and in some respects decisive. There is no question but that the Left Opposition must do all it can to penetrate into the life of the Jewish workers. . . .

QUESTION: In the Jewish circles you are considered to be an "assimilator." What is your attitude towards assimilation?

TROTSKY: I do not understand why I should be considered an "assimilator." I do not know, generally, what meaning this word holds.

I am, it is understood, opposed to Zionism and all such forms of self-isolation on the part of the Jewish workers. I call upon the Jewish workers of France to better acquaint themselves with the problems of French life and of the French working class. Without that it is difficult to participate in the working-class movement of that country in which they are being exploited.

As the Jewish proletariat is spread in different countries it is necessary for the Jewish worker, outside of his own language, to strive to know the language of other countries as a weapon in the class struggle.

What has that to do with "assimilation"?

QUESTION: The official Communist Party [in the US] characterized, without question, the Jewish-Arab events in 1929 in Palestine as the revolutionary uprising of the oppressed Arabian masses. What is your opinion of this policy? [EDITOR: In August 1929 Arab gangs targeted Jews in Hebron and elsewhere in Palestine, during which more than 130 Jews were murdered. In addition, 116 Arabs were killed, most of them shot by the British imperialist police. The Stalin-led Communist International and its parties in the US and elsewhere hailed this anti-Jewish pogrom as a revolutionary rebellion.]

TROTSKY: Unfortunately, I am not thoroughly familiar with the facts to venture a definite opinion. I am now studying the question.

Then it will be easier to see in what proportion and in what degree there were present those elements such as national liberationists (anti-imperialists) and reactionary Mohammedans and anti-Semitic pogromists.

On the surface, it seems to me that all these elements were there.

QUESTION: What is your attitude about Palestine as a possible Jewish "homeland" and about a land for the Jews generally?

TROTSKY: Both the fascist state in Germany, as well as the Arabian-Jewish struggle, bring forth new and very clear verifications of the principle that the Jewish question cannot be solved within the framework of capitalism.

I do not know whether Jewry will be built up again as a nation. However, there can be no doubt that the material conditions for the existence of the Jewish people as an independent nation could be brought about only by the proletarian revolution.

There is no such thing on our planet as the notion that one has more claim to land than another.

The establishment of a territorial base for the Jewish people in Palestine or any other country is conceivable only with the migrations of large human masses. Only a triumphant socialism can take upon itself such tasks. It can be foreseen that it may take place either on the basis of a mutual understanding, or with the aid of a kind of international proletarian tribunal that should take up this question and solve it.

The blind alley in which the Jewish people of Germany find themselves, as well as the blind alley in which Zionism finds itself, is inseparably bound up with the blind alley of world capitalism as a whole. Only when the Jewish workers clearly see this interrelationship will they be forewarned against pessimism and despair.

CHAPTER 4

Continuing Lenin's course in face of Stalinist counterrevolution

The political battle to keep the Communist International and its parties on a proletarian internationalist course to extend the world socialist revolution was initiated by V.I. Lenin in 1922–23. Lenin sought support from Leon Trotsky above all in this enormous undertaking, and it was Trotsky who carried on and led that fight after Lenin's death in 1924.

The challenges of leading the Communist International were inextricably intertwined with the consolidation and advances of the young Bolshevik-led Soviet republic. The revolutionary government worked from the outset to establish a federation of equals joining proletarian Russia with the oppressed peoples long encased in the former tsarist prison house of nations, which stretched from present-day Ukraine to the Pacific Ocean.

Such a union could only be achieved by the *voluntary* action of those peoples, whose unconditional right to national self-determination was recognized by the new government.

By 1922 more than twenty autonomous republics and regions had decided to become part of such a voluntary union. Lenin, however, objected to Joseph Stalin's proposal that these nations "enter" the existing Russian Soviet Federated Socialist Republic, established soon after the revolution. Instead, Lenin insisted, Russians would join with other nationalities "on an equal basis into a new union, a new federation," which in December 1922 became the Union of Soviet Socialist Republics (USSR). Stalin grudgingly acquiesced to what he called the Bolshevik leader's "unimportant amendments," reflecting the "national liberalism of Comrade Lenin."

Acting over coming years to advance rising bureaucratic layers in the Soviet government and Communist Party, Stalin pursued a counterrevolutionary course that elevated the interests of these privileged social layers over those of the toilers and other nationalities. In order to serve the interests of that bureaucratic caste, Stalin abandoned Lenin's proletarian internationalist course of subordinating the interests of Soviet Russia to strengthening revolutionary working-class and anticolonial struggles elsewhere in the world.

As part of this political counterrevolution against Lenin and Bolshevism, Stalin and the privileged layers he represented used Jew-hatred more and more openly and ruthlessly.

'I declare war on Great Russian chauvinism'

MEMORANDUM TO THE POLITICAL BUREAU

V.I. LENIN, OCTOBER 1922

I declare war to the death on Great Russian chauvinism.[1] I shall eat it with all my healthy teeth as soon as I get rid of this accursed bad tooth.

It must be *absolutely* insisted that the [Soviet Union's] Central Executive Committee should be *presided over* in turn by a Russian, Ukrainian, Georgian, etc.

Absolutely!

Lenin's letter on the national question to the Twelfth Party Congress

LYDIA FOTIEVA, APRIL 1923

The following letter was written by Lydia Fotieva, Lenin's personal secretary, to Lev Kamenev with a copy to Leon Trotsky, both of whom were Political Bureau members of the Communist Party of the Soviet Union. Fotieva refers here to Lenin's unpublished December 31, 1922, "article on the national question," which was in fact part of a letter to the upcoming twelfth party congress, an excerpt from which follows in this chapter. Due to strokes in December 1922 and March 1923, Lenin couldn't present his views to the delegates himself, as he had initially planned.

When the congress opened April 17, 1923, its presiding committee rejected giving delegates Lenin's views on the national question (or anything else from the letter) and ruled that it not be discussed. Instead, the congress adopted a resolution presented by Stalin that—with no mention of Lenin's views— warned against "a new theory to the effect that the Great Russian proletariat must be placed in a position of inequality in relation to the former oppressed nations." None of Lenin's proposals were either made known to delegates or acted on.

To Comrade Kamenev (copy to Comrade Trotsky):[2]

To round out our telephone conversation, I am informing you, as acting chairman of the Political Bureau, of the following:

As I already told you, on December 31, 1922, Vladimir Ilyich dictated an article on the national question.

This question has worried him extremely, and he was preparing to speak on it at the party congress. Not long before his last illness he told me that he would publish this article, but later. After that he took sick without giving final instructions.

Vladimir Ilyich considered this article to be a guiding one and extremely important. At his direction it was communicated to Comrade Trotsky, whom Vladimir Ilyich authorized to defend his point of view upon the given question at the party congress in view of their solidarity upon it.

The only copy of the article in my possession is preserved at Vladimir Ilyich's instructions in his secret archive.

I bring the above facts to your attention.

I could not do it earlier since I returned to work only today after a sickness.

◆

'Not the slightest crudity or injustice toward other nationalities'

FROM LETTER TO TWELFTH PARTY CONGRESS

V.I. LENIN, DECEMBER 1922

The harm that can result to our state from a lack of unification between the national apparatuses and the Russian apparatus is infinitely less than that which will be done not only to us but to the whole International and to the hundreds of millions of the peoples of Asia, which are destined to follow us onto the stage of history in the near future.[3]

It would be unpardonable opportunism if, on the eve of the debut of the East, just as it is awakening, we undermined our prestige with its peoples, even if only by the slightest crudity or injustice toward our own non-Russian nationalities. The need to rally against the imperialists of the West, who are defending the capitalist world, is one thing. There can be no doubt about that and it would be superfluous for me to speak about my unconditional approval of it.

It is another thing when we ourselves lapse, even if only in trifles, into imperialist attitudes towards oppressed nationalities, thus undermining all our principled sincerity, all our principled defense of the struggle against imperialism. But the morrow of world history will be a day when the awakening peoples oppressed by imperialism are finally aroused and the decisive long and hard struggle for their liberation begins.

The program of international revolution or socialism in one country

FROM 'DRAFT PROGRAM OF THE
COMMUNIST INTERNATIONAL,
A CRITICISM OF FUNDAMENTALS'

LEON TROTSKY, 1928

In our epoch, which is the epoch of imperialism, i.e., of world economy and *world* politics under the hegemony of finance capital, not a single communist party can establish its program by proceeding solely or mainly from conditions and tendencies of developments in its own country.[4] This also holds entirely for the party that wields the state power within the boundaries of the USSR.

On August 4, 1914, [the opening guns of the first imperialist world war] the death knell sounded for national programs for all time. The revolutionary party of the proletariat can base itself only upon an international program corresponding to the character of the present epoch, the epoch of the highest development and collapse of capitalism.

An international communist program is in no case the sum total of national programs or an amalgam of their common features. The international program must proceed directly from an analysis of the conditions and tendencies of world economy and of the world political system taken as a whole in all its connections and contradictions, that is, with the mutually antagonistic interdependence of its separate parts.

In the present epoch, to a much larger extent than in the past, the national orientation of the proletariat must and can flow only from a world orientation and not vice versa. Herein lies the basic and primary difference between communist internationalism and all varieties of national socialism. . . .

We have kept insisting upon these considerations since 1923–24, when the question of the United States of America arose in its full scope as a problem of *world* and, in the most direct sense of the term, of *European* politics. . . .

America's *new* role in Europe since the capitulation of the German Communist Party, and the defeat of the German proletariat in 1923, has been left absolutely unevaluated. No attempt at all has been made to explain that the period of the "stabilization," "normalization," and "pacification" of Europe as well as the "regeneration" of the social democracy, has proceeded in close material and ideological connection with the first steps of American intervention in European affairs. . . .

No mention at all has been made of the fact (and this is just as important a phase of the same world problem) that it is precisely the international strength of the United States and her irresistible expansion arising from it, that compels her to include the powder magazines of the whole world into the foundations of her structure, i.e., all the antagonisms between the East and the West, the class struggle in Old Europe, the uprisings of the colonial masses, and all wars and revolutions.

On the one hand, this transforms North American capitalism into the basic counterrevolutionary force of the modern epoch, constantly more interested in the maintenance of "order" in every corner of the terrestrial globe; and on the other hand, this prepares the ground for a gigantic revolutionary explosion in this already dominant and still expanding world imperialist power. The logic of world relations indicates that the time of this explosion cannot lag very far behind that of the proletarian revolution in Europe. . . .

If in the past decade the main source of revolutionary situations lay in the direct consequences of the imperialist war, in the second postwar decade the most important source of revolutionary upheavals will be the interrelations of Europe and America. A major crisis in the United States will strike the tocsin for new wars and revolutions.

We repeat: there will be no lack of revolutionary situations. The entire question hinges upon the international

The Communist and Socialist Parties' betrayals of workers struggles paved the way for the imperialist slaughter of World War II and the Nazi Holocaust.

TOP: Berlin, 1933. Nazi storm troopers seize union headquarters. When German Communist Party refused to form united front with Social Democrats to defeat Nazi terror, fascists seized power and crushed workers movement without a fight.

CENTER: Spain, 1936. Workers form militias to defend republic against fascist revolt led by Gen. Francisco Franco. Revolution was defeated after leaders of Stalinist CP subordinated struggles of working people to a Popular Front government coalition with SP and liberal capitalists and landowners.

BOTTOM: France, May 1936. Workers occupy Renault auto plant, part of wave of sit-down strikes by 2 million workers that threatened to topple capitalist government. Communist and Socialist Parties joined Popular Front government and called for "social harmony" with bosses, demobilizing revolutionary upsurge.

party of the proletariat, the maturity and fighting ability of the Comintern, and the correctness of its strategical position and tactical methods.

◆

The Stalinist regime is reviving the anti-Semitic traditions of tsarism

FROM INTERVIEW WITH 'JEWISH DAILY FORWARD'

LEON TROTSKY, JANUARY 1937

What distinguishes the new [1936 Soviet] constitution from the old one [1924] is the attempt *to strengthen and perpetuate the vast economic privileges and absolute dictatorship of the Soviet bureaucracy.*[5]

You ask me about the trial of the sixteen. On this matter I am now finishing a small book, in which I hope to prove to every critical and honest person that the Moscow trial represents the greatest falsification in the political history of the whole world. Such historically well-known trials as the famous Beilis trial in tsarist Russia, the trial of Dreyfus in France, the Reichstag fire trial in Germany, are child's play compared to the trial of the sixteen. And new trials are coming up....

The more the privileges of the Soviet ruling caste grow, the more sharply must it suppress every voice of criticism and opposition. It cannot, however, openly punish its opponents before the eyes of the people for demanding more equality and more freedom. It is compelled to bring false accusations against the Oppositionists. It was clear to me as early as 1927 that the bureaucracy would pin various horrible crimes on the Opposition, and that it would have to stifle the independence of the popular masses so that the truth would not burst through.

To develop these thoughts, I wrote on March 4, 1929: "There remains only one thing for Stalin: to try to draw a line of blood between the official party and the Opposition. *He absolutely must connect the Opposition with terrorist crimes, preparation of armed insurrection, etc.".* . .

You ask me whether there is a connection between the Moscow trial and anti-Semitism. Absolutely!. . . Whoever attentively follows the inner life of the Soviet Union, whoever reads the Soviet press line by line and between the lines, has for a long time clearly seen that the Soviet bureaucrats are playing a double game on the Jewish question, as on other questions.

In words, of course, they come out against anti-Semitism; bigoted pogromists are not only brought to court by them but also shot. At the same time, though, they systematically exploit anti-Semitic prejudices in order to compromise every Opposition group. In the commentaries on the political trial proceedings, about the artistic taste of the defendants, about the character of their social position, there is always and invariably the hint that the Opposition is an outgrowth of the Jewish intelligentsia.

It should be said openly: on this plane the Stalinist bureaucracy has revived in a more polite form the tradition of the tsarist bureaucracy. The economic and cultural development of all other nationalities of the Soviet Union also suffers from the dictatorship of the Bonapartist bureaucracy.

"The Stalinist bureaucracy revived the anti-Semitism of the tsarist regime."
—Leon Trotsky, 1937

TOP: Stalin regime staged 1936–38 Moscow frame-up trials, which sentenced to death central leaders of Bolshevik Revolution, including Leon Trotsky, then in exile in Mexico. Many defendants were portrayed as "lawless Jews" selling themselves to Nazi regime. Here, 1937 anti-Semitic cartoon published by Soviet regime portrays "Judas Trotsky."

CENTER: Socialist Workers Party exposed Moscow trials in party press, December 1937.

BOTTOM: In infamous 1953 "Doctors' Plot," nine physicians, six of them Jews, were imprisoned on fake charges of conspiring to murder Soviet leaders. Soviet magazine *Krokodil* portrayed them in anti-Semitic caricature. Shortly after Stalin's death in March 1953 the case was dropped.

The attempts to represent me and my cothinkers as enemies of the Soviet Union are absurd and dishonest. I do not confuse the Soviet Union with the bureaucratic caste that has developed. I believe in the future of the Soviet Union, which will liberate itself from the bureaucracy and will complete the business begun by the October Revolution. . . .

On the Jewish question, first of all, I can say that it cannot be resolved within the framework of the capitalist system, nor can it be resolved by Zionism. At one time I thought that the Jews would assimilate into the peoples and cultures they lived among. This was the case in Germany and even in America, and for this reason it was possible to make such a prediction.

But now it is impossible to say this. Recent history has taught us something about this. The fate of the Jews has been posed as a burning question, particularly in Germany, and the Jews who had forgotten their ancestry were clearly reminded of it. I foresee a similar situation developing in France, where there are already signs of strong anti-Semitic currents, not to mention the sharp manner in which the Jewish question has been handled in the Eastern European capitalist countries in the last few years.

If capitalism continues to survive for a long time, the Jewish question will be posed in the same sharp way in all the countries where Jews live, including the USA.

I cannot say what will become of the Jews in a few hundred years, just as I do not know what will become of the Mexicans. I do know, however, that the Jewish question will only be resolved by the socialist revolution. I am talking about the Jewish question in general terms, because I know little about the internal problems of Jewish life. I can say, however, that under the socialist order, the Jews, too, can and should lead their own lives as a people, with their own culture, which has undergone a profound development in recent years.

The territorial question is pertinent because it is easier for a people to carry out an economic and cultural plan when it lives in a compact mass. Under socialism that question will arise, and with the consent of those Jews who desire it, there might be a free mass emigration, which no one would be forced to join, just as in general there will be no rule by force in the socialist state. For if a group of Jews maintain that they wish to live under socialism in the Jewish culture, which makes it possible for them to live in accordance with their own way and their own spirit, then why shouldn't they be able to do this?

Concentration in a compact place is necessary for cultural development, because this makes it easier to extend cultural influence to broad masses through a strong mass-circulation press, theater, etc. If Jews desire this, socialism will have no right to deny it to them. I want to underline that I am not saying that Jews must have a territory, because under socialism the Jews, like other peoples, will be free and secure to live wherever they reside.

The Jewish question in all its ramifications can, however, only be resolved by the proletarian revolution. For this reason, the Jewish working masses should work with and fight alongside the workers of all countries for the accomplishment of this goal.

◆

Setbacks to revolution breed unbridled chauvinism and Jew-hatred

LEON TROTSKY, FEBRUARY 1937

The privileged bureaucracy, fearful of its privileges, and consequently completely demoralized, represents at present *the most antisocialist and most antidemocratic stratum of Soviet society.*[6] In the struggle for its self-preservation it exploits the most ingrained prejudices and the most benighted instincts. If in Moscow, Stalin stages trials which accuse the Trotskyites of plotting to poison the workers, then it is not difficult to imagine to what foul depths the bureaucracy can resort in some Ukrainian or central Asiatic hovel! ...

In order to demonstrate more sharply to the workers the differences between the "old" course and the "new," the Jews, even when unreservedly devoted to the general line, were removed from responsible party and Soviet posts. Not only in the country but even in Moscow factories the baiting of the Opposition back in 1926 often assumed a thoroughly obvious anti-Semitic character. Many agitators spoke brazenly: "The Jews are rioting."

I received hundreds of letters deploring the anti-Semitic methods in the struggle against the Opposition. ... In the months of preparations for the expulsions of the Opposition from the party, the arrests, the exiles (in the second half of 1927), the anti-Semitic agitation assumed a thoroughly unbridled character.

The slogan "Beat the Opposition," often took on the complexion of the old slogan "Beat the Jews and save Russia." The matter went so far that Stalin was constrained to come out with a printed statement which declared: "We fight against Trotsky, Zinoviev, and Kamenev not because they are Jews but because they are Oppositionists," etc.

To every politically thinking person it was completely clear that this consciously equivocal declaration, directed against "excesses" of anti-Semitism, did at the same time with complete premeditation nourish it. "Do not forget that the leaders of the Opposition are—Jews." That was the *meaning* of the statement of Stalin, published in all Soviet journals....

The physical extermination of the older generation of the Bolsheviks is, for every person who can think, an incontrovertible expression of Thermidorian reaction, and in its most advanced stage at that. History has never yet seen an example when the reaction following the revolutionary upsurge was not accompanied by the most unbridled chauvinistic passions, anti-Semitism among them....

Our descendants will know better than we what to do. I have in mind a transitional historical period when the Jewish question, as such, is still acute and demands adequate measures from a world federation of workers' states. The very same methods of solving the Jewish question which under decaying capitalism have a utopian and reactionary character (Zionism), will, under the regime of a socialist federation, take on a real and salutary meaning. This is what I wanted to point out.

How could any Marxist, or even any consistent democrat, object to this?

◆

The struggle against imperialism and war

FROM 'THE DEATH AGONY OF CAPITALISM AND
THE TASKS OF THE FOURTH INTERNATIONAL'

LEON TROTSKY, SEPTEMBER 1938

In 1938 Leon Trotsky collaborated with leaders of the Social-
ist Workers Party in drafting the program of a new revolution-
ary International, a program grounded in the deeds and words
of the Third International led by Lenin.

"The Death Agony of Capitalism and the Tasks of the Fourth
International," an excerpt from which follows, was the title of
that programmatic document, which was adopted by the Sep-
tember 1938 founding conference of that new international
organization. It is more commonly known as "The Transitional
Program for Socialist Revolution."

Before exhausting or drowning mankind in blood, capitalism befouls the world atmosphere with the poisonous
vapors of national and race hatred.[7] Anti-Semitism today
is one of the more malignant convulsions of capitalism's
death agony.

An uncompromising disclosure of the roots of race prejudice and all forms and shades of national arrogance and
chauvinism, particularly anti-Semitism, should become
part of the daily work of all sections of the Fourth International, as the most important part of the struggle against
imperialism and war.

Our basic slogan remains: Workers of the World Unite!

CHAPTER 5

Forging a proletarian party in the United States: The 1930s and World War II

During the global capitalist economic and social crisis of the 1930s and US capital's buildup toward the second imperialist world slaughter, Leon Trotsky, then living in exile in Mexico, collaborated closely with the Socialist Workers Party leadership in the struggle to build a proletarian party in the United States. Those leadership efforts were part and parcel of a broader political struggle in the international communist movement.

By the mid-1930s, confidence and militancy among workers in the US was growing, as employment turned up from rock-bottom levels at the start of the decade. Union organizing drives were being fought and won in more and more basic industries, resulting in the explosive rise of the new industrial union federation, the CIO (Congress of Industrial Organizations).

As elsewhere in the world, as these struggles posed a threat to bourgeois stability and class rule, fascist groups emerged in the US, with a base especially among insecure petty bourgeois layers. With growing encouragement from employers, these fascist outfits targeted trade unions, working-class parties, and Jews.

The most advanced response to this menace came from the powerful Teamsters Union Local 544 in Minneapolis. The local's central leadership, who were also leaders and cadres of the SWP, had led the workers who won the 1934 Teamster strikes that made Minneapolis a union town, and then reached out from there to organize a quarter million over-the-road truck drivers into the union.

In August 1938 Local 544 initiated a broadly based union defense guard that decisively defeated the bosses' attempt in Minneapolis to use the Silver Shirts, a US fascist group, to break the Teamsters union and victimize Jews.

Workers and trade unionists in New York, New Jersey, and elsewhere sought collaboration from the Teamsters leadership to combat union-busting and Jew-hatred by fascist forces in their areas. That collaboration helped lay the groundwork for a mass demonstration of some 50,000 working people and others in New York City that in February 1939 countered a pro-Nazi rally of 20,000 inside Madison Square Garden.

Below Farrell Dobbs, a central leader of the class-struggle labor vanguard in Minnesota and of the SWP, recounts how the Local 544 Union Defense Guard stopped the Silver Shirts. The excerpt is from *Teamster Politics*, the third of Dobbs's four-volume account of these working-class battles in the 1930s and their lessons.

❖

Workers self-defense,
not reliance on the bosses' state

FROM 'TEAMSTER POLITICS'

FARRELL DOBBS

Clashes between capital and labor in times of social crisis tend to stimulate activity among political demagogues with a fascist mentality.[1] They anticipate that intensification of the class struggle will cause sections of the ruling class to turn away from parliamentary democracy and its methods of rule, and resort to fascism as the way to hold on to state power and protect special privilege. Each of the aspirants hopes, moreover, to be chosen as the "fuehrer" to lead the terrorist movement needed for the murderous assault on the working class that accompanies such a turn in policy.

Several of these would-be Hitlers had, in fact, come forward in this country in the early 1930s, but they made little headway in the period marked by the stormy rise of the CIO. Then, during 1937–38, the situation began to change. A second deep economic slump developed, marking the collapse of Roosevelt's New Deal. Social contradictions in general grew sharper, as the ruling class prepared to plunge the country into the impending imperialist war.

The bureaucratic misleaders in the trade unions failed to guide the workers toward a meaningful course for coping with difficulties caused by these developments—formation of an independent labor party. And in those circumstances significant numbers of demoralized middle-class elements in the cities, impoverished farmers, and to a certain extent unemployed workers fell prey to ultraright hucksters.

As a result various profascist groups that had sprung up earlier began to recruit quite rapidly, and they received a parallel increase in financial backing from wealthy antilabor interests. Emboldened by this new support, they became more aggressive, as well as more provocative. In some instances these outfits organized uniformed bands of storm troopers, which were drilled openly; and whether uniformed or not, thugs of that type were mobilized to launch terror campaigns, initially directed at the most vulnerable targets, but aimed basically at organized labor.

Jewish people were among the first to be attacked. As in Nazi Germany, they were made scapegoats in an effort to intensify anti-Semitic prejudices against them, the primary object being to sow division in the working class. But they weren't the only victims.

Lone worker-militants were waylaid and beaten in New York and other eastern cities. Street meetings of left-wing groups were broken up. In Jersey City the notorious Mayor Frank Hague engineered hoodlum assaults on union meetings and picket lines; and in New Orleans a Teamster strike was crushed by vigilantes. As the latter events showed, the ultraright forces that were engaged in these terrorist acts on behalf of the capitalists were rapidly zeroing in on their main target—the mass organizations of the working class.

One of these profascist groups, the Silver Shirts of America, was of special concern to General Drivers Union, Local 544. It was started in 1932 by William Dudley Pelley, who opened a headquarters in Asheville, North Carolina, and published a weekly organ called *Liberation*. Tacitly conceding jurisdiction over the major cities to other ultrarightists,

Pelley centered his efforts on the towns and countryside of the farming areas. Although little was achieved in that sphere during the first years, the Silver Shirts had at last begun to make gains.

Apparently this caused a section of the boss class in Minneapolis to become interested in the movement; and Pelley was encouraged to send one of his aides, Roy Zachary, to the city in the summer of 1938 to launch an organizing drive. Two Silver Shirt rallies followed in quick succession, on July 29 and August 2, at the Royal Arcanum hall. These affairs were closed to the public, admission being by invitation only.

Despite the secrecy, the Teamsters had gotten wind of Zachary's arrival in town and had kept him under close scrutiny. Knowledge of the planned rallies was gained beforehand, making it possible to arrange a way to get reliable intelligence as to what happened.

Thus it became known immediately that Zachary's main theme had been to call for a vigilante attack on the headquarters of Local 544.

It was also learned that literature was passed out at both meetings inviting the participants to join F.L. Taylor's "Associated Council of Independent Unions." Taylor, by the way, had already shown his fascist inclinations a few weeks earlier when he set out to form a vigilante force under the name "Minnesota Minute Men." So it was perfectly natural for him to hook up with the Silver Shirts when they moved in.

A short time later another ominous fact was revealed by Rabbi Gordon, a religious opponent of fascism, who had also been keeping track of Zachary's doings. Gordon announced that George K. Belden, head of the Associated

Mr. Belden and the Silver Shirts

The August 11, 1938 issue of The Northwest Organizer, *the Minneapolis Teamsters' weekly newspaper, featured a front-page editorial with the above headline. Below are its opening and closing paragraphs.*

Thanks to Rabbi Gordon, the fact has become public that George K. Belden, head of the Associated Industries, personally participated in meetings of the Silver Shirts, the fascist organization which is preparing to carry out armed raids on union halls.

When Rabbi Gordon made public copies of letters he had sent Belden and the Associated Industries, these had no choice except to try to lie their way out of the situation as gracefully as they might. The Associated Industries passed the buck by saying that its chieftain had attended the Silver Shirt meetings "merely" as an individual. Belden said the same thing and added that he had attended just "out of curiosity." Then he sought to get out of it by the hoary old subterfuge of every Jew-baiter and reactionary, namely, that he had some Jewish friends and therefore, presumably, did not unqualifiedly stand for the Jew-baiting of the Silver Shirts....

The main point is: BELDEN IS PLANNING TO USE FASCIST THUGS AGAINST THE TRADE UNIONS.

On Guard!

On Guard, brothers and sisters of the trade union movement! Guard well the portals of your unions against the fascist danger. Keep your eyes open everywhere for signs of the fascist storm troops. Prepare to deal with

> them as they deserve to be dealt with. Let every trade
> unionist say: "We shed our blood and gave our martyrs
> to build our unions; we'll fight to the death to keep our
> unions."

Industries, had attended both Silver Shirt rallies. When questioned about this by the press, Belden told a reporter for the *Minnesota Leader*: "I am in sympathy with getting rid of racketeers...."

Taken as a whole, these developments added up to a dire threat against the Teamsters. A fink union that had dragged Local 544 into court was now tied in with the Silver Shirts; Belden's role showed that the employers were directly involved in the new antiunion plot; and talk of an armed raid on the Teamster headquarters was in the air.

This situation called for prompt countermeasures. So Local 544, acting with its customary decisiveness, answered the threat by organizing a union defense guard during August 1938.

Formation of the guard was reported in the *Northwest Organizer*, and a press release announcing the step was handed to the daily papers, which gave it prominent mention. The new body's functions were described in the report as "defense of the union's picket lines, headquarters and members against anti-labor violence." Through this action the local served public notice that it would take care of its own defense, putting no misplaced reliance on the police for protection.

The union leaders were fully aware that capitalist politicians in seats of power not only tend to wink at fascist hooliganism; they often encourage and abet such extralegal attacks on workers. Not only that. Their minions, the police, condone and protect fascist activities, become members of such movements and, when open violence is used against the trade unions, usually look the other way. Such had been the conduct of capitalist "forces of law and order" in Germany, Italy, and other places; history taught that the situation would be no different in the United States.

An iron necessity was thus imposed upon the workers. If they were to defend themselves, they had to use their own organizations for the purpose. In that respect Local 544's pioneer action in forming a union defense guard not only served its own needs; the step blazed a trail for trade unionists everywhere in the country.

Conceptually, the guard was not envisaged as the narrow formation of a single union. It was viewed rather as the nucleus around which to build the broadest possible united defense movement. From the outset, efforts were made to involve other unions in the project. It was expected that time and events could also make it possible to extend the united front to include the unemployed, minority peoples, youth—all potential victims of the fascists, vigilantes, or other reactionaries.

For these reasons the defense formation was not made an official part of Local 544. Instead, it was initiated by leading members of the local, acting with the approval of the general membership. A spontaneous recruitment process was set into motion through a series of meetings with groups of workers. In this way the main base of the guard was quickly established by the General Drivers; and after that its ranks were gradually extended to include members of other unions in the city that approved the idea.

The guard was in no sense an elite body. It was simply a businesslike formation open to any active union member. The only requirements for inclusion in its ranks were readiness to defend the unions from attack, willingness to take the necessary training for that purpose, and acceptance of the democratic discipline required in a combat unit. Moreover, its activities were conducted only with the consent of the membership of the trade unions involved, and under their control.

As in the case of Local 544 itself, the guard functioned democratically in its internal affairs. Steps taken to carry out its assigned tasks were decided through open discussion and majority vote. This procedure was also used in selecting leaders who were to have command authority during any combat.

Ray Rainbolt of the Local 544 staff was elected commander in chief of the defense formation. He had impressive credentials. Besides his extensive know-how in leading trade-union struggles, he had acquired considerable military knowledge during earlier hitches in the US army.

Those chosen as lower-ranking officers had likewise proven themselves in the class struggle and won recognition as secondary union leaders. Similarly, in the case of the guard's rank and file, all had been battle tested to one extent or another in strike actions. Taking the body as a whole, there were numerous military veterans with various abilities developed in the armed forces. Among them were former sharpshooters, machine gunners, tank operators, and so on. Quite a few had been noncommissioned officers. One had been a signal corps officer and still another an officer in the German army.

Structurally, the body was divided into small units to facilitate rapid mobilization in the event of a surprise attack on the union movement. Squads of five were the norm, with a member of each squad being designated captain. In a relatively short time the force thus organized was built up to about six hundred.

Members of the guard were issued small lapel emblems bearing the legend "544 UDG," which they were encouraged to wear at all times. When on duty they used large armbands prominently marked "544 Union Defense Guard" to identify themselves. This designation was readily accepted by those from other unions who were part of the formation, because they realized that use of the prestigious number 544 gave the name added meaning.

The organization raised its own funds—for purchases of equipment and to meet general expenses—by sponsoring dances and other social affairs. Part of this money was used to buy two .22 caliber target pistols and two .22 caliber rifles to give guard members a way to improve their ability to shoot straight. Regular practice sessions were then held for that purpose. In addition, periodic drills were scheduled to provide training in defensive tactics.

Members of the guard were not armed by the unions, since in the given circumstances that would have made them vulnerable to police frame-ups. But many of them had guns of their own at home, which were used to hunt game; and those could quickly have been picked up if needed to fight off an armed attack by Silver Shirt thugs.

At the drill sessions, lectures were given on tactics used in the past by antilabor vigilantes in this country and fascists abroad. Discussions were then held to work out defensive measures to meet attacks of the kind.

An intelligence department was also set up. Its task was to keep a lookout for fascist and anti-Semitic literature and activities, fink propaganda, and the like. One particular episode graphically illustrated the breadth of the intelligence arm, as well as the guard's effectiveness in action. It came about when the Silver Shirts attempted to hold another rally, to be addressed by Pelley himself.

On the day of the scheduled affair a cab driver delivered Pelley to a residence in the city's silk-stocking district.

The driver immediately reported this to Rainbolt, who telephoned the place and warned that Pelley would run into trouble if he went ahead. To show he was not bluffing, Rainbolt led a section of the union guard to Calhoun Hall, where the rally was to be held that night. Arrival of the union forces caused the audience to leave in a hurry, and the demagogue never did show up. Then, around midnight, another cab driver called Rainbolt to report that he had just dumped Pelley at the Milwaukee depot in time to catch a night train to Chicago.

Following that incident the Teamsters took a step calculated to throw a further scare into the would-be union busters. It came in the form of a special notice printed on the front page of the *Northwest Organizer* of September 29, 1938. The notice instructed all captains of the defense guard to have their squads up to full strength forthwith and to be prepared to mobilize them, ready for action, on short notice.

The move seemed to have the desired effect, for the Silver Shirts transferred their next meeting to the neighboring city of St. Paul. It was held on October 28 at the Minnehaha Hall, and the place was well guarded by cops. Zachary was the main speaker. As reported in the newspapers the next morning, he boasted:

"Leaders of 544 have said we cannot hold meetings in Minneapolis, but we shall hold them, with the aid of the police. The police know that someday they'll need our support and that's why they're supporting us now."

Zachary's line was taken seriously by the Teamsters for several reasons. More could have been involved in the St. Paul affair than a mere effort to boost the sagging morale of the profascist elements by holding a successful meeting. Part of the scheme could also have been to bring pressure upon the Minneapolis authorities to provide them with comparable police protection in that city as well. If so, Associated Industries was in all likelihood involved in the maneuver.

Acting on such assumptions, the high command of the union defense guard decided to put on a public show of force. The aim was twofold: to make it plain to one and all that the Silver Shirts were not going to operate in Minneapolis without a serious fight and, simultaneously, to test the guard's efficiency in the course of such a demonstration.

Toward those ends an emergency mobilization of the defense formation was called on one hour's notice. Only three people knew what was up. As part of the test all others were left with the impression that a real crisis had developed. By the designated assembly time, just sixty minutes after the call first went out, about three hundred members of the guard had turned out ready for action—an impressive performance.

The mobilization took place on a vacant plot of land in the center of the city, so a lot of people would see what was going on. Once the men were assembled there, Rainbolt explained that it had been a practice operation to give yet another warning to the Silver Shirts and their supporters among the employers. A clinical discussion was then held about the results of the test.

Since all kinds of personal plans for the evening had been rudely upset, a bit of entertainment was in order by way of compensation. So the guard was marched in a long column—armbands prominently displayed—to a downtown burlesque theater, where a block of seats had been reserved.

As for the ultrarightists, they appeared to have gotten the union's message loud and clear. Zachary made no further attempts to hold rallies in Minneapolis; fascist propaganda tapered off; and after a time it became evident that the Silver Shirt organizing drive in the city had been discontinued altogether.

Despite this favorable turn in the situation, the union defense guard was maintained as a form of insurance against any resurgence of the fascist threat. But the nature of its activities underwent a change. Target practice and drill sessions were tapered off. Gradually the guard's functions shifted mainly to monitoring union picnics and other large social gatherings. Through occasional public displays of this kind the antilabor forces were reminded of the continued existence of the defense formation.

On balance, Local 544 had not only warded off another capitalist attack. The experience with the Silver Shirts had given many of its members a better understanding of the need for workers self-defense, and the best militants had gained deeper insight into the laws of class struggle.

"Clashes between capital and labor in times of crisis stimulate demagogues with a fascist mentality. They aim to lead murderous assaults on the working class."
—*Farrell Dobbs*

TOP: Minneapolis, 1934. Striking Teamsters defend unionists from cop attack. Workers' battles made Minneapolis a union town and organized a quarter million over-the-road drivers into Teamsters in much of the Midwest.

CENTER: During Great Depression, pro-fascist groups began to emerge in the US. The Silver Shirts, led by William Pelley, launched a recruitment drive in Minneapolis.

BOTTOM: Minneapolis, 1938. Union Defense Guard initiated by Teamsters Local 544. It defeated bosses' attempt to use Silver Shirts to bust up unions and victimize Jews.

LEFT: November 1938 protest in New York, sponsored by Socialist Workers and others, called on Washington to open doors to the refugees. Action was called after *Kristallnacht* (Night of broken glass), when Nazi storm troopers rounded up 30,000 Jews and destroyed Jewish businesses and synagogues across Germany.

ABOVE: February 1939, New York. Mobilization of 50,000 workers called by Socialist Workers Party against pro-Nazi meeting of 20,000 at Madison Square Garden.
INSET: February 24, 1939, *Socialist Appeal*.

Our course on the Jewish question:
The international class struggle

THESES ON THE JEWISH QUESTION

SWP POLITICAL COMMITTEE, 1938

A few months after the US communist movement took on its current form as the Socialist Workers Party at the opening of 1938, the party's Political Committee adopted a resolution on the Jewish Question. In November, the SWP National Committee issued a declaration in response to the Nazis' Kristallnacht *pogroms across Germany earlier that month. That call to action launched the campaign the party organized and led—before, during, and after World War II—demanding that Washington open the doors to Jews seeking refuge from Nazi persecution. Excerpts from these two SWP documents appear below.*

Our approach to the Jewish question can be none other than that of the international class struggle.[2] In its death agony the capitalist class maintains itself in power by resorting to unmitigated brutality and violence aimed at the working class, particularly at its vanguard. It utilizes every element of hatred and prejudice which it can fan into flame to bring about division among the masses and to establish a social basis for its fascist, gangster rule.

The Jews, by virtue of the fact that everywhere they form only a small minority of the population, and because anti-Semitism has always been fostered, sometimes openly, sometimes in masked form, constitute an easy scapegoat upon whom the big bourgeoisie can divert the pent-up, dangerous wrath of the backward elements among the masses, and particularly of the desperate middle classes. The fascist hirelings of the big bourgeoisie use the most vicious, lying propaganda to inflame to pogrom temperature the dormant antagonism to the Jews.

Precisely because the fomenting of anti-Semitism has become an inseparable part of the technique of fascist reaction, the revolutionary party has a double duty to perform in combating it. It has the duty of exposing the real aims of the capitalists, hidden behind the smokescreen of anti-Semitism and thereby inoculating the masses against the poison; it has also the special task of mobilizing the real defense of the persecuted Jews, a defense of necessity based on the might of the organized working class. If these tasks are properly carried out, then we can at the same time hope to attract to our firm support the Jewish masses....

The Transitional Program includes the necessity for building workers' defense groups. This idea can find especially fertile soil for implanting and for growth into reality among the Jewish masses.

It goes without saying that such defense groups constituted under our influence must not consist of Jews alone. Nevertheless, we must take full advantage of the great concentration of the Jews in New York City to enlist as many as possible in such defense organizations. In this respect the situation in Jersey City [with its incipient fascist, union-busting, Jew-hating gangs organized by Democratic Party mayor Frank Hague] and its implications for the Jews need hardly be emphasized.

Jewish organizations must be encouraged to set up defense groups, which should be offered aid by workers' organizations. Similarly we must exert our influence wherever possible to have workers' defense groups come to the aid of the Jews when necessary.

◆

Open the doors to refugees from Hitler's Nazi terror!

FROM SOCIALIST WORKERS PARTY 'CALL TO ACTION'

SWP NATIONAL COMMITTEE, NOVEMBER 1938

The entire world has been shocked to the depths by the outburst of a new campaign of brutal violence against the Jews in Germany [the Kristallnacht pogroms of November 9–10, 1938].[3]

The hideous terror of Hitlerism has never struck with such cruel and merciless force.

Throughout Germany, bands of Nazi gangsters organized and commanded by their leaders, have wrecked and looted stores owned by Jews. Jewish synagogues have been burned and destroyed by the instructed fascist mobs. The workers of Germany, who hate and despise Hitlerism with all their strength, were unable to come to the aid of the brutalized Jews because they are themselves still in the straitjacket of the Nazi terror.

The brown-shirted monsters do not even bother to conceal their aim: the physical extermination of every Jew in Great Germany.

Already a "fine" has been levied against the Jews, which means in effect the complete confiscation of all their property and its distribution among the Nazi sadists.

The regime of the ghetto is to be restored in Germany by the complete segregation of all Jews into marked-off slums. With this measure, Hitlerism shows again that it means barbarism, the destruction of all civilized progress, the return to the shame and depravity of the Middle Ages.

Why are the Hitlerites increasing their murderous attack upon the Jews?

For two reasons:

They hope to take the minds of the German workers and peasants off the misery from which they suffer, to make them think that the Jews—traditional scapegoats for reaction—are responsible for all their ills.

They hope to blackmail the international protest movement against fascism into cowardly silence.

If they accomplish these dastardly aims, they can continue without the slightest opposition their rule of blood and iron.

If they accomplish their aims, they will encourage the fascist reaction in every other country of the world to advance more boldly, more insolently, more successfully.

They must not be allowed to succeed! . . .

WE THEREFORE DEMAND:

Throw open the doors of the United States to the victims of the Hitlerite pogrom regime!

We urge all workers and other labor organizations:

Demand that the American government use its emergency powers to open the doors to the horribly persecuted Jews of Germany! . . .

Show the victims of the fascist terror that you mean it seriously, by stretching out to them the hand of fraternal solidarity, by demanding of the American government the free and unrestricted right of asylum for the Jewish scapegoats of fascist barbarism!

◆

Protect workers meetings and Jews menaced by fascist hoodlums

FROM TESTIMONY AT MINNEAPOLIS SEDITION TRIAL

JAMES P. CANNON, NOVEMBER 1941

In December 1941 eighteen leaders of the Socialist Workers Party and Local 544-CIO (formerly Teamsters) were convicted on federal charges of "conspiracy to advocate the overthrow of the government by force and violence." The thought-control Smith Act, under which they were sent to federal prison for up to sixteen months, had been signed into law by Democratic Party President Franklin Roosevelt only months earlier in 1940 and was used for the first time in this frame-up trial.

Above all, Washington aimed to silence forces such as the leadership of Local 544 and the SWP who were conducting propaganda among working people for a labor party based on the unions and campaigning against the US rulers' rationalizations for dragging them into the unfolding imperialist war.

The central defendant was James P. Cannon, SWP national secretary at the time and a founding leader of the Communist Party in 1919. His testimony was first published in the book Socialism on Trial *in 1942. In the excerpts below, under questioning from his attorney Albert Goldman, Cannon testified about why the SWP calls for workers defense guards.*

GOLDMAN: Now, with reference to the workers defense guard advocated by the Socialist Workers Party, what formal action did the party take at any time?[4]

CANNON: Well, in this later period of 1938 and '39, in some parts of the country we were confronted with an incipient fascist movement. Different organizations with different names began preaching Hitlerite doctrines in this country, and tried to practice Hitlerite methods of physical intimidation of workers meetings, of Jews, Jewish stores, and suppressing free speech by violent methods.

In New York it became a rather acute problem. The various Bundists [thugs of the Nazi-inspired German-American Bund] and associated groups in New York developed the practice of breaking up street meetings when either our party or some other workers party would attempt to speak under a permit given by the city authorities. They had a habit of going around and molesting Jewish storekeepers, picketing them, and beating them, and challenging them to fight, and so on.

There was an organization rampant at that time called the "Silver Shirts." I don't recall them in New York, but at various points in the West and Midwest.

GOLDMAN: Do you recall the Christian Front?

CANNON: Yes, in New York the Bundists and the Christian Front, and two or three other would-be fascist organizations used to combine on this kind of business. At this time free speech was being very flagrantly denied in Jer-

The Socialist Workers Party fought for political independence of unions from the capitalist state, for a labor party based on the unions, and against Washington's war preparations.

TOP: Defendants Farrell Dobbs (left) and James P. Cannon during Minneapolis frame-up trial, in which 18 leaders of Socialist Workers Party and Teamsters Local 544 were sentenced to federal prison under thought-control Smith Act. Washington sought to silence those such as SWP and Teamsters leaders who were conducting propaganda for a labor party and against bosses' rapacious war aims.

CENTER: July 26, 1941, *Militant* explains why Roosevelt administration was prosecuting the socialists.

BOTTOM: Sit-down strike at General Motors auto assembly plant in Flint, Michigan, 1937. It was part of strike wave during 1930s Depression that built Congress of Industrial Organizations and posed potential for workers to organize independently of bosses in political arena.

sey City under the authority of this man [Democratic Party mayor Frank] Hague who announced that he was the law, got the habit of chasing people out of town and permitting meetings to be broken up ostensibly not by the authorities, but by the "outraged citizens" whom he and his gang had organized for that purpose.

In general there were signs then—there was a lot of discontent and unrest in the country—there were signs of a fascist movement growing up, and the question arose of how we could protect, not only ourselves, but how could the unions protect themselves. For example, in Jersey City picketing was denied by these means and the right to strike infringed upon—very serious questions of the invasion of civil liberties by unofficial bodies.

Basing ourselves on the experiences of the German and Italian fascist movements, which began with gangs of hoodlums and ended by destroying completely the labor unions and all workers organizations and all civil rights—we came to the conclusion that the fascists should be met on their own ground, and that we should raise the slogan of workers defense guards to protect workers meetings, halls and institutions against hoodlum violence by the incipient fascists.

We discussed that with Trotsky; his part in it was primarily an exposition of the development of the fascist movement in Europe. I don't recall now whether he originated the idea, but at any rate he heartily seconded it, that our party should propose that the unions, wherever their peace was menaced by these hoodlums, should organize workers defense guards and protect themselves.

GOLDMAN: And did the unions follow the advice of the party?

CANNON: I recall that we organized, in cooperation with some other radicals and some Jewish people—even some Jewish nationalists who didn't agree with our socialist program, but agreed on defending their human rights to live— we formed at that time a workers defense guard in New York. To protect not only the meetings of our party but of any organization menaced by these hoodlums. To protect citizens from molestation in the Bronx, where these hoodlums were intimidating and insulting Jewish people. This guard had several scuffles and fights with these gangs.

Then conditions in the country began to change. The economic situation in the country improved a bit. The question of the European war began to absorb attention, and take it away from these provincial American Hitlers. The fascist movement dropped into passivity and our workers defense guard in New York didn't have anything to do and it just passed out of existence. In Los Angeles, if I recall correctly, there was a similar experience.

GOLDMAN: Did any international trade unions ever adopt that idea, as far as you know?

CANNON: I don't know. I know the question was raised in the Garment Workers Union, which had a double concern about the matter because, first, as a labor union they were menaced by the growth of fascism, and second, a large percentage of their members are Jews, who are considered proper victims by these hoodlums.

A resolution was passed in favor of the idea in one of the garment locals in New York, and was referred then to the International Executive Board for consideration, and some correspondence and some interviews between our comrades who had sponsored the idea and the officers of the

International Ladies' Garment Workers Union took place. I don't think it developed any further, either positively or negatively, because the fascist movement subsided and the issue got cold.

GOLDMAN: So that the issue of the workers defense guard died down because a change of conditions occurred?

CANNON: Yes. We retained the proposal for workers defense guards in our program. I believe it is on the editorial page of the *Militant* as one of the points we are proposing as a practical program.

GOLDMAN: And it becomes vital especially in view of a possible fascist movement in our country?

CANNON: Yes. At that time our paper was full of stories and articles about the Bundists and the Christian Fronters, and so on, but if you look over the files, they show a gradual recession of reports about fascist violence. And the question of the workers defense guard left the pages of the paper and is only occasionally raised there now in a slogan.

The witness: (continuing)—I might add, Mr. Goldman, that so far as I know, there doesn't exist now any functioning workers defense guard in any part of the country that our members are associated with, not to my knowledge. But we retain the idea for practical education in case the unions should again encounter the experience of those days.

The task is to create a
defense guard in the trade unions

FROM DISCUSSIONS WITH SWP LEADERS

LEON TROTSKY, JUNE 1938

In June 1938 Leon Trotsky held a second round of discussions with Socialist Workers Party leaders to discuss the program he was drafting with the party leadership's collaboration for the founding conference of a new international revolutionary organization. Trotsky was living in forced exile in Mexico at the time.

Among the topics was the need for the SWP to encourage the unions to initiate and organize workers defense guards against the bosses' hired thugs and fascist gangs targeting the labor movement, Jews, and others. The excerpt below is from the transcript of that meeting.

QUESTION: How do we go about launching the defense groups practically?[5]

TROTSKY: It is very simple. Do you have a picket line in a strike? When the strike is over, we say we must defend our union by making this picket line permanent.

QUESTION: Does the party itself create the defense group with its own members?

TROTSKY: The slogans of the party must be placed in quarters where we have sympathizers and workers who will defend us. But a party cannot create an independent defense organization. The task is to create such a body in the trade unions.

We must have these groups of comrades with very good discipline, with good, cautious leaders, not easily provoked, because such groups can be provoked easily. The main task for the next year would be to avoid conflicts and bloody clashes. We must reduce them to a minimum with a minority organization during strikes, during peaceful times. In order to prevent fascist meetings it is a question of the relationship of forces. We alone are not strong, but we propose a united front....

In Minneapolis, where we have very skilled, powerful comrades, we can begin to show the entire country.

◈

The fight against fascism begins in the factory and ends in the street

FROM THE TRANSITIONAL PROGRAM FOR SOCIALIST REVOLUTION

LEON TROTSKY, 1938

Sit-down strikes are a serious warning from the masses, addressed not only to the bourgeoisie but also to the organizations of the workers, including the Fourth International.[6] In 1919–20, the Italian workers seized factories on their own initiative, thus signaling to their "leaders" the news of the coming of the social revolution. The "leaders" paid no heed to the signal. The victory of fascism was the result....

The sharpening of the proletariat's struggle means the sharpening of the methods of counterattack on the part of capital. New waves of sit-down strikes can and undoubtedly will call forth resolute countermeasures on the part of the bourgeoisie. Preparatory work is already being done by the confidential staffs of big trusts. Woe to the revolutionary organizations, woe to the proletariat if it is again caught unawares!

The bourgeoisie is nowhere satisfied with the official police and army. In the United States, even during "peaceful" times, the bourgeoisie maintains militarized battalions of scabs and privately armed thugs in factories. To this must now be added the various groups of American Nazis. The French bourgeoisie at the first approach of danger mobilized semilegal and illegal fascist detachments, including such as are in the army. No sooner does the pressure of the English workers once again become stronger, than immediately the fascist bands are doubled, trebled, increased tenfold to come out in bloody march against the workers.

The bourgeoisie keeps itself most accurately informed about the fact that in the present epoch the class struggle irresistibly tends to transform itself into civil war. The examples of Italy, Germany, Austria, Spain, and other countries taught considerably more to the magnates and lackeys of capital than to the official leaders of the proletariat.

The politicians of the Second and Third Internationals, as well as the bureaucrats of the trade unions, consciously close their eyes to the bourgeoisie's private army; otherwise, they could not preserve their alliance with it for even twenty-four hours. The reformists systematically implant in the minds of the workers the notion that the sacredness of democracy is best guaranteed when the bourgeoisie is armed to the teeth and the workers are unarmed....

The struggle against fascism does not start in the liberal editorial office but in the factory—and ends in the street. Scabs and private gunmen in factory plants are the basic nuclei of the fascist army. *Strike pickets* are the basic nuclei of the proletarian army. This is our point of departure. In connection with every strike and street demonstration, it is imperative to propagate the necessity of creating *workers' groups for self-defense....*

It is necessary to give organized expression to the valid hatred of the workers toward scabs and bands of gangsters and fascists. It is necessary to advance the slogan of a *workers' militia* as the one serious guarantee for the inviolability of workers' organizations, meetings, and press.

Only with the help of such systematic, persistent, indefatigable, courageous agitational and organizational work, always on the basis of the experience of the masses themselves, is it possible to root out from their consciousness the traditions of submissiveness and passivity; to train detachments of heroic fighters capable of setting an example to all toilers; to inflict a series of tactical defeats upon the armed thugs of counterrevolution; to raise the self-confidence of the exploited and oppressed; to compromise fascism in the eyes of the petty bourgeoisie and pave the road for the conquest of power by the proletariat.

Engels defined the state as bodies of "armed men." *The arming of the proletariat* is an imperative concomitant element to its struggle for liberation. When the proletariat wills it, it will find the road and the means to arming. In this field, also, the leadership falls naturally to the sections of the Fourth International.

CHAPTER 6

The Socialist Workers Party in the fight against Jew-hatred and pogroms today

As news of the October 7, 2023, pogrom became known, the Socialist Workers Party and its cothinkers in Communist Leagues in other countries were on the front lines of actions condemning the most murderous assault on Jews since the Holocaust during World War II.

The statement below was issued by Rachele Fruit, currently the 2024 SWP candidate for president of the United States, at an October 10 response by 3,000 at the Holocaust memorial in Miami. It continues to stand as the essential working-class course of action.

◈

To end Jew-hatred, fight to win workers power and socialism

SOCIALIST WORKERS PARTY CAMPAIGN STATEMENT

RACHELE FRUIT, OCTOBER 10, 2023

In the fight against Jew-hatred and pogroms, the Socialist Workers Party's continuity is rooted in Lenin and the Bolshevik Revolution in Russia.[1] Socialists can never support any crime against humanity in the name of revolution.

Working people cannot rely on imperialist democracies to protect Jews. Washington and London closed the door on Jewish immigration before, during and after the Second World War. That fact, together with the betrayal by the Stalinists in Moscow and elsewhere of revolutionary opportunities in China, Germany, France, and Spain, led to Hitler's "Final Solution."

That's why Israel had to be, and has to exist as, a refuge for the Jews.

Those who call themselves "socialists," and who champion Hamas and other terrorist proxies of Iran, will easily find themselves allied with future fascist forces.

Only the working classes of Israel, Palestine, Iran, and the entire region can find a solution in their common interests. And the same is true for workers in the United States and the world over.

The Socialist Workers Party is today on the front lines in the fight against Jew-hatred.

MARGARET TROWE/MILITANT

ERIC SIMPSON/MILITANT

LEFT: Laura Garza, Socialist Workers Party candidate for US Senate in California, and campaign supporters join thousands marching in San Francisco to protest rise in incidents of Jew-hatred in the area, March 3, 2024.

NAOMI CRAINE/MILITANT

ABOVE: Striking members of United Auto Workers rally in Detroit, September 2023. Some 25,000 unionists struck GM, Ford, and Stellantis plants in 21 states. They made gains in wages and job conditions, encouraging workers across the US facing attacks on their living standards.

The low point of labor resistance is behind us, says 2022 SWP resolution.

Workers power: The indispensable political weapon to combat all oppression

FROM 'MALCOLM X, BLACK LIBERATION, AND THE ROAD TO WORKERS POWER'

JACK BARNES

As proven by the class struggle in the twentieth century and opening decades of the twenty-first, Jew-hatred and genocidal violence against Jews are neither a European question nor a Middle Eastern question. They are a world question, a class question, a permanent feature of the imperialist epoch.

"Now more than ever," wrote Leon Trotsky, "the fate of the Jewish people—not only their political but also their physical fate—is indissolubly linked with the emancipating struggle of the international proletariat."[2] That conclusion is just as applicable to October 7, 2023, as to the world Trotsky was describing in December 1938.

At the predawn of the imperialist epoch, industrial and banking capital in the United States consolidated their dominance in the decades following the US Civil War and abolition of chattel slavery, the Second American Revolution. In 1877, across the states of the defeated southern slavocracy, postwar Radical Reconstruction was crushed in blood. The entire working class suffered what remains the worst setback in its history.

Blacks were by far the major victims of lynchings and other vigilante mobs during the subsequent decades of Jim Crow terror. But Jews, Catholics, and Chinese were targets, as well.

Nearly a century later, the massive proletarian-based movement that overturned Jim Crow in the 1950s and 1960s dealt a powerful blow against Jew-hatred and all forms of oppression.

In 1877 the US rulers withdrew federal troops from the states of the old Confederacy.[3] These troops had been the armed force of last resort standing between the freed Black toilers, on the one hand, and gangs of well-armed reactionary vigilantes, on the other. Throughout the closing decades of the nineteenth century and well into the twentieth, successive generations of organizations such as the Knights of the White Camelia, the White League, the Ku Klux Klan, the White Citizens Councils, and many others—named, unnamed, or renamed—carried out an unrelenting reign of terror against the Black population in the South.

This systematic violence helped the capitalists drive toilers who were Black into virtual peonage as sharecroppers and tenant farmers, and made it possible for Jim Crow segregation to be imposed and codified into state law in one southern state after another. These gangs were also organized to break the spirit of any class-conscious worker or farmer anywhere in the South who wasn't Black—"nigger lovers"—and to prevent them from linking arms with toilers who were Black in common struggles for land, for public education, for cheap credit and railway rates, for labor union rights, or anything else in the interests of the oppressed and exploited. Anti-Catholic, anti-Chinese, and anti-Semitic prejudice and discrimination reached new heights.

Working people can and will wrest concessions from the ruling class in the course of sharpening struggles against the crisis-fueled assaults on our jobs, living conditions, and elementary human dignity, on our political liberties and

The proletarian-based movement that overturned Jim Crow segregation in the US also dealt a blow to Jew-hatred and all forms of oppression.

TOP: Mass meeting launches 1955–56 boycott of city buses in Montgomery, Alabama, a key battle in struggle that overthrew Jim Crow system of racial segregation in US South. The SWP joined campaign urging unionists to donate station wagons to maintain transportation for those boycotting the buses.

CENTER: Malcolm X speaks to youth in Selma, Alabama, standing up to brutal cop attacks and racist violence, February 4, 1965. Malcolm became the face and voice of the forces of the coming American revolution.

BOTTOM: Leo Frank, a Jewish factory manager in Atlanta, was lynched by a Jew-hating mob in 1915. He had been framed up on charges of raping and murdering a 13-year-old worker. White supremacist terror groups like the Ku Klux Klan organized lynchings of Blacks and spewed Jew-hatred.

right to unionize, and against the march toward increased military spending and bloodier wars abroad.[4] But these concessions cannot alter the laws underlying the operations of the capitalist system itself or forestall its further devastation of our lives and livelihoods. They cannot end the dictatorship of capital.

Only the conquest, and exercise, of state power by the working class and expropriation of finance capital can lay the foundations for a world based not on exploitation, violence, racial discrimination, class-based pecking orders, and dog-eat-dog competition, but on solidarity among working people that encourages a lifetime of creativity and recognizes the worth of every individual, regardless of sex, national origin, or skin color.

A socialist world.

What does any socialist revolution open up for the oppressed and exploited?[5] Above all, it opens the possibility of *using* the state power of the dictatorship of the proletariat, which is far and away the most powerful instrument fighting toilers can ever wield, to advance the battle to eradicate racism, national oppression, women's second-class status....

What the conquest of workers power does is make available to a mass vanguard of the proletariat the most effective political weapon in history—one we can use to battle all forms of oppression and lay the basis to establish human solidarity on new, communist foundations. *That's* the challenge and the promise of the dictatorship of the proletariat: *Win* it, then *wield* it—to *finish* the job.

And acting to help advance revolutionary struggle worldwide is *the way* to finish the job.

◆

A party whose integrity, norms, and conduct correspond with its working-class aims

FROM 'THE LOW POINT OF LABOR RESISTANCE IS BEHIND US'

SOCIALIST WORKERS PARTY RESOLUTION, ADOPTED BY DECEMBER 2022 CONVENTION

The Socialist Workers Party is building and recruits to a proletarian cadre whose character, trustworthiness, norms, and habits of conduct—whose "way of life and activity," as succinctly put in the 1847 rules of the world's first communist organization—correspond with the party's aims and with its unconditional claim to loyalty and discipline from every member.[6]

The norms of conduct set by Farrell Dobbs and others in the class-struggle leadership of the Midwest Teamsters battles, and by Malcolm X in his revolutionary political evolution during the final period of his life, are examples to learn from and emulate. There are no better resources helping us do so than Dobbs's four-volume Teamsters series and his two-volume *Revolutionary Continuity: Marxist Leadership in the U.S.*, as well as *Malcolm X, Black Lib-*

eration, and the Road to Workers Power by SWP national secretary Jack Barnes.

The Socialist Workers Party is building a proletarian cadre whose character, trustworthiness, norms, and habits of conduct correspond with the party's political aims. That's the party we recruit to.

Drawing from the history of class struggles in the US and worldwide, Barnes underscores the programmatic lessons through which Malcolm "became the face and the authentic voice of the forces of the coming American revolution." Above all, the course presented in *Malcolm X, Black Liberation, and the Road to Workers Power,* Barnes notes, is a product of "the disciplined efforts" of Socialist Workers Party cadres—Black, Caucasian, and others—"who have been leading the work since the mid-1970s to build a party that is working class in composition as well as program and action," and "who, in their lives and activity, remain true to their revolutionary convictions to this day."

The cadre of a revolutionary working-class party must be educated in and politically internalize the Marxist program, organizational principles, and history of the proletarian internationalist course of the SWP and world communist movement. That programmatic bedrock is presented in:

• "The Draft Program of the Communist International: A Criticism of Fundamentals," Trotsky's 1928 document published in *The Third International after Lenin*. It is, as James P. Cannon said in his 1929 introduction, "a document of conflict written in the fires of the struggle to preserve [in the Communist International] the fundamental teachings of Marx and Lenin and maintain the proletarian dictatorship of the Soviet Union."

For more than six decades, Washington has sought to punish Cuba's working people for the audacity of making a socialist revolution, which set a powerful example for workers in the US of what we're capable of achieving.

TOP: Havana, April 16, 1961. Fidel Castro addresses mass rally on eve of US-organized mercenary invasion of Cuba, which was defeated in 72 hours. "This is the socialist and democratic revolution of the working people, with the working people, and for the working people," Castro said.

BOTTOM: Cuban and Angolan combatants at Cuito Cuanavale, Angola, where South African army suffered decisive defeat, 1988. Over 16 years, 425,000 Cuban volunteers served in Angola, helping defend its independence from invasions by white-supremacist regime in Pretoria. From the beginning, Cuban Revolution has set example of proletarian internationalism.

• *The Transitional Program*, the 1938 founding resolution of the Fourth International drafted by Trotsky in close collaboration with the Socialist Workers Party leadership. The world communist movement, our program says, "uncompromisingly gives battle to all political groupings tied to the apron-strings of the bourgeoisie. Its task—the abolition of capitalism's domination. Its aim—socialism. Its method—the proletarian revolution."

• *In Defense of Marxism*, the compilation of articles and letters by Trotsky to SWP leaders during the 1939–40 political struggle in the party against a petty bourgeois opposition bending to US imperialism's intensifying war drive. In it, Trotsky presents the Marxist theoretical, programmatic, and organizational reasons why, in his words, "The class composition of the party must correspond to its class program."

• The political importance of a parallel work, *The Struggle for a Proletarian Party* by James P. Cannon, was emphasized by Trotsky in an April 1940 letter to Farrell Dobbs. "Jim's pamphlet … is the writing of a genuine workers leader," Trotsky wrote. If the political struggle against the petty bourgeois opposition in the party "had not produced more than this document, it would be justified."

• *Their Trotsky and Ours* by Jack Barnes, based on a December 1982 talk presented to a public meeting of one thousand in Chicago as part of a socialist educational conference held in conjunction with the Young Socialist Alliance national convention. The talk was given during the opening years of the turn to industry, Barnes later wrote, when "the Socialist Workers Party was becoming more proletarian in composition—in daily life—as well as in program."

Those were years, Barnes wrote, when "the unfolding revolutions in Central America and the Caribbean were

All methods are good that raise workers' consciousness, their trust in their own forces

In a society based upon exploitation, the highest morality is that of the social revolution. All methods are good which raise the class-consciousness of the workers, their trust in their own forces, their readiness for self-sacrifice in the struggle.

The impermissible methods are those which implant fear and submissiveness in the oppressed in the face of their oppressors, which crush the spirit of protest and indignation or substitute for the will of the masses—the will of the leaders; for conviction—compulsion; for an analysis of reality—demagogy and frame-up. That is why the Social Democracy, prostituting Marxism, and Stalinism, the antithesis of Bolshevism, are both mortal enemies of the proletarian revolution and its morals.

To face reality squarely; not to seek the line of least resistance; to call things by their right names; to speak the truth to the masses, no matter how bitter it may be; not to fear obstacles; to be true in little things as in big ones; to base one's program on the logic of the class struggle; to be bold when the hour for action arrives—these are the rules of the Fourth International.

—Leon Trotsky, The Transitional Program for Socialist Revolution (1938) underlining for us once again how, with working-class leadership, the toilers can use a workers and farmers government to advance toward the expropriation of the exploiters and oppressors, the establishment of the dictatorship of the proletariat." Years when "we could see and understand more richly and act with greater confidence on the continuity of our program and strategy" going back to Marx and Engels and the conquests of the Communist International under the leadership of Lenin and the Bolsheviks.

Grounded in these programmatic foundations, every party cadre can more deeply and more concretely internalize and act on the resolution adopted by our 1965 convention, *The Organizational Character of the Socialist Workers Party*. "The party strives for political homogeneity in the sense that admission to its ranks requires fundamental agreement with its program and principles," the resolution states. "For similar reasons unconditional loyalty and disciplined conduct are required as a condition of membership."

Our experiences in the United States since the 2017 party convention confirm that the low point of working-class and labor resistance is behind us. There are more than ample opportunities to continue organizing and acting on our communist course, helping to build the nucleus of a class-struggle left-wing leadership in the unions, and recruiting to the Socialist Workers Party.

If you agree, join us!

Hamas in its own words: Jew-hatred, genocide, anticommunism

Whatever opinion an individual might have of Hamas and of its bloody anti-Jewish massacre of 1,200 people October 7, 2023, anyone calling for an Israeli government cease-fire is in fact falling in step with the propaganda campaign planned in detail by its leaders long before the slaughter and carried out ever since.

Hamas's reactionary aim? To survive another day and keep on slaughtering Jews in Israel.

Hamas ruled Gaza, a de facto state, for almost two decades. It busted unions, arrested and tortured Palestinian political opponents, and denied women any semblance of equal rights. It ran the state, in the words of its own leaders, as "cover" to prepare assaults on Israel and the Jews.

Hamas is trained, financed, and aided in planning its assaults by the counterrevolutionary bourgeois-clerical regime in Tehran. Hamas was joined in its butchery, torture, and sexual outrages October 7 by Islamic Jihad, the Popular Front for the Liberation of Palestine, and other groups. None of them is a liberation organization of the Palestinians or anyone else among the oppressed and exploited.

Everything Hamas does is aimed at annihilating the Jews and destroying Israel.

Below is what Hamas says for itself.

◆

FROM HAMAS'S FOUNDING 1988 COVENANT

Our struggle against the Jews is very great and very serious. It needs all sincere efforts. It is a step that inevitably should be followed by other steps. The Movement is but one squadron that should be supported by more and more squadrons from this vast Arab and Islamic world, until the enemy is vanquished and Allah's victory is realized.... (*Introduction*)

"The Day of Judgment will not come about until Muslims fight the Jews (killing the Jews), when the Jew will hide behind stones and trees. The stones and trees will say O Muslims, O Abdullah, there is a Jew behind me, come and kill him."... (*Article 7*)

They strived to amass great and substantive material wealth, which they devoted to the realization of their dream. With their money, they took control of the world media, news agencies, the press, publishing houses, broadcasting stations, and others.

With their money they stirred revolutions in various parts of the world with the purpose of achieving their interests and reaping the fruit therein. They were behind the French Revolution, the Communist revolution, and most of the revolutions we heard and hear about, here and there....

They were behind World War I, when they were able to destroy the Islamic Caliphate, making financial gains and controlling resources. They obtained the Balfour Declaration, formed the League of Nations through which they could rule the world.

They were behind World War II, through which they made huge financial gains by trading in armaments, and paved the way for the establishment of their state. It was they who instigated the replacement of the League of Nations with the United Nations and the Security Council to enable them to rule the world through them. There is no war going on anywhere, without having their finger in it. (*Article 22*)

The Zionist plan is limitless. After Palestine, the Zionists aspire to expand from the Nile to the Euphrates. When they will have digested the region they overtook, they will aspire to further expansion, and so on. Their plan is embodied in the "Protocols of the Elders of Zion," and their present conduct is the best proof of what we are saying. (*Article 32*)

◆

FROM 2017 HAMAS DOCUMENT
OF GENERAL PRINCIPLES AND POLICIES

The establishment of "Israel" is entirely illegal and contravenes the inalienable rights of the Palestinian people....There shall be no recognition of the legitimacy of the Zionist entity....

Hamas believes that no part of the land of Palestine shall be compromised or conceded, irrespective of the causes, the circumstances, and the pressures and no matter how long the occupation lasts. Hamas rejects any alternative to the full and complete liberation of Palestine, from the river to the sea. (*Articles 18–20*)

◈

Ghazi Hamad
Member, Hamas Political Bureau

FROM INTERVIEW ON LEBANESE TV,
OCTOBER 29, 2023

GHAZI HAMAD: "Everything we do is justified."

The October 7 operation "is just the first time, and there will be a second, a third, a fourth."

QUESTION: "Does that mean the annihilation of Israel?"

HAMAD: "Yes, of course."

"We are proud to sacrifice martyrs."

◈

Mousa Abu Marzouk
Member, Hamas Political Bureau

FROM INTERVIEW ON 'RUSSIA TODAY',
OCTOBER 27, 2023

QUESTION: Many people are asking: Since you have built 500 kilometers of tunnels, why haven't you built bomb shelters, where civilians can hide during bombardment.

MOUSA ABU MARZOUK: We have built the tunnels because we have no other way of protecting ourselves [Hamas] from being targeted and killed.… Everybody knows that 75 percent of the people in the Gaza Strip are refugees, and it is the responsibility of the United Nations to protect them.

Later Marzouk added to BBC Arabic: "Do you expect me to fit 2.5 million people in the tunnels?"

Khaled Mashaal
Founding leader of Hamas and member of its Political Bureau

FROM INTERVIEW ON KUWAITI PODCAST,
JANUARY 2024

"We have nothing to do with the two-state solution. We reject this notion, because…you are required to recognize the legitimacy of the other state, which is the Zionist entity.

"This is unacceptable."

The fascist roots of Hamas lie in Hitler's "Final Solution"

TERRY EVANS

Workers looking to understand why Hamas thugs and their backers in Tehran organized the systematic slaughter of over 1,200 Jews on October 7, 2023, as well as a few dozen Bedouin Arabs and immigrants, will benefit from a look at the group's origins and history.[1] It revolves around their determination "to solve the Jewish question" by exterminating the Jews.

Hamas's forerunners and program lie in ultrareactionary Arab forces that formed a years-long alliance with Hitler's Nazi Party in the 1930s based on a common desire to carry out the "Final Solution"—the slaughter of Jews worldwide. These forces include Amin al-Husseini, who became the grand mufti of Jerusalem in 1921, as well as the Muslim Brotherhood in Egypt (from which, decades later, Hamas emerged in Palestine). These reactionary currents were a byproduct of the deepening worldwide capitalist crisis and the revolutions and counterrevolutions that led to World War II.

Massacres of Jews in the Middle East by Islamist forces began decades before Israel came into existence. The record of these pogroms by Hamas's forerunners are hidden today by the Stalinists and middle-class leftists, who mis-represent Hamas as a national liberation movement, part of the "Palestinian resistance."

Beginning in the early 1920s Amin al-Husseini, a member of one of the top landowning families in Palestine, orchestrated a number of massacres of Jews, both there and as far away as Baghdad. The capitalist rulers in the United Kingdom had taken control of Palestine as part of the notorious Sykes-Picot Agreement, a backroom deal coming out of the imperialist First World War that redrew the borders of lands and peoples in the region (Arabs, Kurds, Jews, and others) and divided the riches of the Middle East between London and Paris.

Al-Husseini's assaults on Jews took place as revolutionary struggles against colonial oppression and capitalist exploitation spread worldwide in the decades following the 1917 Bolshevik Revolution in Russia.

In Egypt a rebellion for independence and a general strike paralyzed British colonial rule in 1919, before London brutally suppressed it.

That same year the Bolsheviks led the formation of the Communist International. Communist parties were soon formed in Egypt and Palestine. In Palestine the party was initially composed of both Jewish and Arab revolutionaries. They strove to emulate the example of the Bolshevik Revolution led by V.I. Lenin by unifying the toilers of all nationalities and religions to take power and open the road to a socialist revolution.

But that promising beginning was destroyed when a political counterrevolution in the Soviet Union led by Joseph Stalin overturned Lenin's proletarian internationalist course in the late 1920s.

In the Middle East this Stalinist reaction led to imposition of a forced "Arabization" on these parties, driving Jews from the leadership and later splitting the organization in Palestine into separate Arab and Jewish parties. On a larger scale, it led to the destruction of the Communist International and its national parties as a revolutionary instrument for the working class everywhere in the world.

Al-Husseini forges ties to Nazi regime

Al-Husseini first led a pogrom in Jerusalem in 1920 during a Muslim religious procession, inciting attacks on the Jewish quarter. The British withdrew their troops from Jerusalem, giving their blessing to the pogrom. Six Jews were murdered and two women raped. The British authorities then pardoned al-Husseini, and appointed him the city's grand mufti, a top religious, legal, and political figure.

In 1929 al-Husseini again urged his followers to attack Jews in Palestine, with more than 130 slaughtered in Hebron and elsewhere. Women were raped and men castrated. British authorities were accountable for most Arab deaths during the 1929 events, and responded by placing limits on Jewish immigration to Palestine.

Britain's rapacious imperialist exploitation in the region was based on playing the Arabs against the Jews in order to control and dominate both (just as it did between Muslims and Hindus in colonial India, resulting in the bloody sectarian division of that country into Pakistan and India in the wake of the successful independence struggle of the 1940s).

By 1937 al-Husseini no longer limited his horizon to elimination of Jews just in Palestine. "Whoever believes that, if the Palestine problem is solved or if the Jews are defeated

Hamas's origins lie in the reactionary Muslim Brotherhood, which formed an alliance with Hitler's Nazi Party in the 1930s, based on a common desire to carry out the "Final Solution" — the slaughter of Jews worldwide.

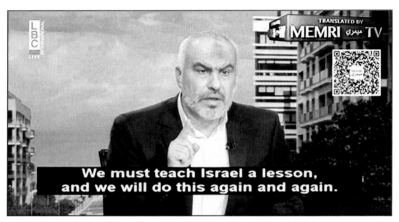

TOP: The October 7, 2023 massacre "is just the first time. There will be a second, a third, a fourth," pledged Hamas leader Ghazi Hamad October 24 on Lebanese TV. "Everything we do is justified."

BOTTOM: Just hours after the bloody pogrom, the Iranian regime's Tasnim News Agency ran this cartoon of missiles raining down on Israel and Jews being driven into the sea—the goal of Hamas and Tehran.

TOP: Berlin, November 1941. Amin al-Husseini, grand mufti of Jerusalem, meets with Adolph Hitler to offer his collaboration "in the struggle against three common enemies: the English, the Jews and Bolshevism." During World War II, Nazis broadcast al-Husseini's Jew-hating tirades by radio across the Mideast.

BOTTOM: November 1943. Al-Husseini salutes Waffen SS troops in Bosnia, where he launched a Muslim division of the Nazi force. After the war, al-Husseini continued to work closely with the Egypt-based Muslim Brotherhood. Four decades later, Hamas was founded as the armed wing of the Muslim Brotherhood in Gaza—with the same goal of exterminating Jews.

in this conflict everything will be fine, are wrong," said the pamphlet *Islam and Judaism*. Authorship of that anonymous Jew-hating screed, which first came off the presses in Cairo in 1937, is generally attributed to al-Husseini. He certainly endorsed it and worked for its wide distribution across Palestine and the Middle East.

A pro-Nazi regime was briefly established in Baghdad, Iraq, in 1941 through an uprising against the British. When the regime collapsed, al-Husseini, who was living in Baghdad at the time, accused the city's substantial Jewish population of being responsible. He helped instigate deadly pogroms that resulted in the murder of nearly 200 Jews all told. The British army had troops based just eight miles away, but chose to do nothing to stop the slaughter.

These assaults proved to be the beginning of the end for Baghdad's Jews, who had comprised around a third of its population. Following the establishment of the state of Israel in 1948, they were terrorized by 1952 into fleeing Iraq almost to a person.

Al-Husseini moved from Baghdad to Berlin in 1941 and operated from there for the rest of World War II. He forged close ties to Hitler and his Nazi regime, working to extend the Holocaust to the Middle East. Al-Husseini assured German foreign minister Joachim von Ribbentrop that Arabs were "the natural friends of Germany because both are engaged in the struggle against three common enemies: the English, the Jews, and Bolshevism."

The Nazis began distributing al-Husseini's writings. Up to the opening of World War II, the German Embassy in Cairo had produced and disseminated Muslim Brotherhood propaganda. Throughout the war, the Nazis broadcast Jew-hating tirades by al-Husseini and others in Arabic,

Farsi, and Turkish via radio, helping spread them to a much wider audience. None of the anti-Hitler Arabic language broadcasts by British or other Allied powers made any effort to politically answer the Nazis' "kill the Jews" vitriol.

Al-Husseini met with Hitler in Berlin in November 1941, concretizing plans for collaboration against Jews in the Middle East. In cooperation with the Nazis, al-Husseini launched a Muslim division of Hitler's hated paramilitary SS in Yugoslavia, recruiting Muslims from Bosnia.

From 1941 to 1943, German field marshal Erwin Rommel led German and Italian forces in an effort to drive British forces out of Egypt, take control of the Suez Canal, and open the door to seizing the region's oil supplies. Al-Husseini's SS was to follow in his trail, tasked with eliminating Jews there.

Rommel's forces made significant gains. When it appeared as though Rommel was on the verge of a decisive breakthrough, al-Husseini put out a call over the air waves from Berlin. "Everywhere people are asking what part they can play in wiping out the British and the Jews," said The Voice of the Free Arabs radio station. "Every Jew's name must be written down, together with his address and his business."

"Arabs of Syria, Iraq and Palestine, what are you waiting for?" the station said twelve days later. "Kill the Jews, burn their property, destroy their stores."

But Rommel was defeated at al-Alamein, Egypt, and Hitler never threatened the Middle East again.

Joins with Muslim Brotherhood

In 1945 Allied forces captured al-Husseini and held him under house arrest in France. He escaped the next year and went to Egypt, where he was feted by the reactionary Muslim Brotherhood, which had just instigated a pogrom in Cairo in which six Jews were murdered.

"Germany and Hitler are gone," said the Brotherhood's central leader, Hassan al-Banna. "But al-Husseini will continue the struggle."

And that's what he did.

Al-Husseini assumed the leadership of the Arab Higher Executive Committee of Palestine, dedicated to blocking the establishment of the state of Israel as a refuge for several hundred thousand Jewish survivors in Europe. He led the effort that, just one day after Israel's declaration of independence in May 1948, resulted in the invasion of the new state by the reactionary governments of Egypt, Iraq, Jordan, Lebanon and Syria. The assault had been defeated by early the next year.

Hamas was founded in 1987 as the armed wing of the Brotherhood in Palestine. Its political lineage goes back to al-Husseini and his collaboration with the Nazi regime.

Hamas shares the same hatred for the Jews as a people and the same desire to see them driven off the face of the earth.

The truth about the historical roots of Hamas shatters the notion that this bloodthirsty group has any claim to being an anti-imperialist or progressive leadership of Palestinian workers and peasants. They are the opposite: a reactionary threat to Palestinian toilers, to the Jews, and to the entire working class, of whatever national origin.

A genocidal murder machine that must be fought and defeated.

SOURCE NOTES

CHAPTER 2

1. From "Anti-Jewish Pogroms," in V.I. Lenin, *Collected Works* (Moscow: Progress Publishers, 1960–70) vol. 29, pp. 252–53. Hereafter *LCW*.

2. From *Lenin on the Jewish Question* (New York: International Publishers, 1974), pp. 141–42.

3. From "Lecture on the 1905 Revolution," in *LCW*, vol. 23, p. 250.

4. From "The Reaction Is Taking to Arms," in *LCW*, vol. 10, pp. 508–512.

5. From "Slogans and Organization of Social Democratic Work Inside and Outside the Duma," in *LCW*, vol. 17, p. 337.

6. From "The National Equality Bill," in *LCW*, vol. 20, pp. 172–73.

7. From Leon Trotsky, *My Life* (Pathfinder, 1970), pp. 458–59.

8. From "Does the Jewish Proletariat Need an 'Independent Political Party'?" in *LCW*, vol. 6, pp. 334–35.

9. From James P. Cannon, *First Ten Years of American Communism* (Pathfinder, 1973), p. 114.

CHAPTER 3

1. From "Report of the Commission on the National and Colonial Questions," in *LCW*, vol. 31, pp. 241–42.

2. From "Preliminary Draft Theses on the National and Colonial Questions," in *LCW*, vol. 31, pp. 148–50.

3. From the February 1934 issue of *Class Struggle*, a magazine edited by Albert Weisbord. Available online at https://www.marxists.org/archive/weisbord/FourTwo.htm

CHAPTER 4

1. From *Lenin's Final Fight: Writings 1922–23* (Pathfinder, 2010), p. 119.

2. From *Lenin's Final Fight*, pp. 356–58.

3. From *Lenin's Final Fight*, p. 243.

4. From Leon Trotsky, *The Third International after Lenin* (Pathfinder, 1996), pp. 25–32.

5. From "Interview with the 'Jewish Daily Forward,'" in *Writings of Leon Trotsky 1936–37* (Pathfinder, 1978), pp. 124–30.

6. From "Thermidor and Anti-Semitism," in the May 1941 *New International*. Available online at https://www.marxists.org/archive/trotsky/1937/02/therm.htm

7. From "The Death Agony of Capitalism and the Tasks of the Fourth International," in Leon Trotsky, *The Transitional Program for Socialist Revolution* (Pathfinder, 1977), p. 172.

CHAPTER 5

1. From Farrell Dobbs, *Teamster Politics* (Pathfinder, 2015), pp. 187–97.

2. From James P. Cannon, *The Founding of the Socialist Workers Party: Minutes and Resolutions 1938–39* (Pathfinder, 1982), pp. 403–4, 410–11.

3. From *The Founding of the Socialist Workers Party*, pp. 415–18.

4. From James P. Cannon, *Socialism on Trial: Testimony at Minneapolis Sedition Trial* (Pathfinder, 2014), pp. 129–133.

5. From *Tribunes of the People and the Trade Unions* (Pathfinder, 2019), pp. 91–92.

6. From Leon Trotsky, *The Transitional Program for Socialist Revolution* (Pathfinder, 1977), pp. 161–63.

CHAPTER 6

1. From the socialist newsweekly the *Militant*, October 23, 2023.

2. Leon Trotsky, "On the Jewish Problem," in *Fourth International*, December 1945. Available online at https://www.themilitant.com/NI/FI45/FI45_12.PDF#page=25&view=FitV,35

3. From Jack Barnes, *Malcolm X, Black Liberation, and the Road to Workers Power* (Pathfinder, 2009), pp. 179–80.

4. From *Malcolm X, Black Liberation, and the Road to Workers Power*, pp. 18–19.

5. From *Malcolm X, Black Liberation, and the Road to Workers Power*, p. 313.

6. From Jack Barnes, Mary-Alice Waters, Steve Clark, *The Low Point of Labor Resistance Is Behind Us: The Socialist Workers Party Looks Forward* (Pathfinder, 2023), pp. 118–22.

APPENDIX

1. From the *Militant*, December 11, 2023.

GLOSSARY

1905 Russian Revolution – Revolution against tsarism by workers, peasants, soldiers began in January. Workers' councils, *soviets,* comprised of factory delegates functioned as provisional government. Tsar Nicholas II decreed parliament with limited powers, the Duma, to undercut revolution. Tsarist-backed pogroms escalated during and after revolution.

Beilis trial – 1913 trial of Menahem Mendel Beilis, a Jew in Kyiv, framed up for killing Christian boy. Trial accompanied by vicious campaign accusing Jews of using human blood for ritual purposes (blood libel). Jury refused to convict.

Belostok – Now Bialystok in Poland. Scene of pogrom in 1906 with scores of Jews murdered.

Black Hundreds – Tsarist-backed league of landowners, rich peasants, and government and church figures who murdered revolutionaries and instigated pogroms during and after 1905 Russian Revolution.

Bolshevik Party – see Russian Social-Democratic Labor Party

Bonapartist – Regime that relies on an authoritarian executive power that presents itself as standing above contending class forces to maintain power of dominant ruling layer.

Bund (General Union of Jewish Workers) – Active between 1897 and 1920; claimed to be sole political representative of Jewish workers. Within Russian Social-Democratic Labor Party, it proposed federated structure and opposed course of Lenin and the Bolsheviks.

Christian Front – A militia-like political organization formed in 1938 after call by Father Charles Coughlin, the anti-Semitic and anticommunist "radio priest." Organized attacks and boycotts of Jewish-owned shops.

Comintern (Communist or Third International) – World organization of Communist movement founded in 1919 under Lenin's leadership. Revolutionary alternative to class-collaborationist Socialist (Second) International.

Cossacks – Cavalry soldiers in Russia and Ukraine who received special privileges and land in return for military service. Among main organizers of anti-Jewish pogroms.

Council of People's Commissars – Chief executive body of Soviet government.

Dreyfus, Alfred (1859–1935) – Jewish army captain in France, target of notorious anti-Semitic frame-up in 1894 as spy for Germany, based on forged evidence. Sentenced to life. Pardoned in 1899 through worldwide defense campaign.

Fourth International – World organization of communist parties founded in 1938 at initiative of Bolshevik leader Leon Trotsky. Became necessary with Third International betrayal of Lenin's proletarian internationalist course.

Gordon, Albert (1903–1968) – Rabbi in Minneapolis 1930–46 and opponent of fascism. Hosted weekly radio program.

Hague, Frank (1876–1956) – Democratic Party mayor of Jersey City 1917–47 with close ties to Roosevelt administration. An incipient fascist figure, in 1930s used mayor's office, police violence, and hired thugs to drive unions out of city and persecute socialists and communists.

Holocaust – Systematic killing of 6 million Jews during World War II by Nazi Germany and its collaborators. Forty percent of the world's 16.6 million Jews were slaughtered between 1941 and 1945 in Hitler's "Final Solution of the Jewish Question."

Kamenev, Lev (1883–1936) – A Bolshevik Party leader; leading figure in Soviet government after 1917. Executed during Stalin's frame-up trials.

Kristallnacht – Pogrom against Jews carried out by Nazi paramilitary forces throughout Germany and territories under its control in November 1938. Known as "Night of Broken Glass" due to destruction of Jewish-owned businesses, synagogues, homes. More than 90 Jews killed and 30,000 Jewish males rounded up and sent to concentration camps.

Left Opposition – Headed by Leon Trotsky and founded in 1923; fought in Russian Communist Party and Communist International to continue Lenin's proletarian internationalist course.

Mein Kampf **(My Struggle)** – Political manifesto, 1925, by Adolf Hitler promoting key components of Nazism: anti-Semitism and plan for Aryan world. Drew on Jew-hating *Protocols of the Elders of Zion.*

Moscow Trials – Show trials staged by counterrevolutionary bureaucracy headed by Stalin, 1936–38. Every member of Political Bureau from Lenin's time was arrested, most executed. Exceptions were Stalin himself and Leon Trotsky, who was forced into exile in 1928 and assassinated by Stalin's secret police in Mexico in 1940.

New Deal – Legislative program initiated in 1933–34 by President Franklin D. Roosevelt aimed at defusing rising working-class resistance and stabilizing capitalist rule.

Northwest Organizer – Newspaper published by Minneapolis Teamsters 1934–42 as voice for fighting labor movement in Upper Midwest. Began as first strike daily ever published by a union in United States.

Nuremberg rallies – Massive Nazi party rallies, held annually 1933–38. Hitler used them to spew anti-Semitic rants.

Opposition – see Left Opposition

Pan-Islamism – Movement originating in late 19th century in Ottoman Empire. Tried to link struggle against European and US colonial rule with strengthening power of nobles, large landowners, and clergy.

Pelley, William Dudley – see Silver Shirts.

Protocols of the Elders of Zion – Anti-Semitic forgery by tsarist secret police of "minutes" of purported secret meetings of Jews, published 1905. Aimed at lending credence to "international Jewish conspiracy" for world domination. Prominently used by Hitler and Nazis, as well as by Hamas.

Reichstag fire – In February 1933 the German parliament building (Reichstag) burned down. Falsely blaming communists for arson, Nazi leaders and allies suspended constitutional protections, began to build concentration camps.

Russian Social-Democratic Labor Party (RSDLP) – founded 1898. In 1903 Lenin and Bolshevik wing charted course as independent party with revolutionary program. Renamed Russian Communist Party (Bolsheviks) in March 1918.

Russian Socialist Federated Soviet Republic (RSFSR) – Established in 1917 after victory of Russian Revolution. RSFSR was largest of four republics in what became in 1922 the Union of Soviet Socialist Republics (USSR), a voluntary union of equal nations.

Silver Shirts – Fascist organization founded by William Dudley Pelley, 1933. Spread Jew-hatred and organized attacks against unions throughout 1930s.

Sit-down strikes, France (May–June 1936) – Wave of strikes and factory occupations that opened prerevolutionary period threatening capitalist rule. Stalinist CP demobilized workers to stabilize bourgeois People's Front government of Socialist Party, CP, and capitalist Radical Party.

Socialist Workers Party (SWP) – Revolutionary workers party in the US. Originated as the US Communist Party (CP) founded 1919. CP members opposing counterrevolutionary course of Stalin were expelled and founded Communist League of America (CLA), 1929. Became Socialist Workers Party, 1938.

Spanish Revolution (1936–1939) – In 1936 fascist forces began civil war. Amid growing capitalist crisis workers and peasants began seizing factories and land. Stalinist CP demobilized in order to strengthen Popular Front Republican government. Revolution ended in defeat and establishment of fascist regime in 1939. With this defeat, World War II became virtually inevitable.

Stalin, Joseph (1879–1953) – Presided over anti-Leninist political counterrevolution within Russian Communist Party, Soviet government, and Comintern after death of Lenin. Rejected Lenin's proletarian internationalist course.

Thermidor – Month in the French calendar (July 1794) when bourgeois reaction overthrew the revolution. A parallel to counterrevolutionary course led by Stalin in Soviet Union.

Third International – see Comintern

"Turkey shoot" (Iraq War 1991) – Toward end of US-led ground invasion of Iraq in early 1991 US military command ordered bombardment and shelling of retreating column of Iraqi tanks and vehicles as well as civilian cars, trucks, and buses, slaughtering thousands. US top brass called the carnage a "turkey shoot." Altogether some 150,000 in Iraq were slaughtered during the two-month war.

COMMUNIST CONTINUITY
AND PROGRAM

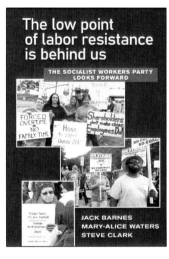

The Low Point of Labor Resistance Is Behind Us

The Socialist Workers Party
Looks Forward

JACK BARNES, MARY-ALICE WATERS
STEVE CLARK

The global order imposed by Washington after its victory in World War II is shattering. A long retreat by the working class and unions has come to an end. The bosses and their government are stepping up attacks on our wages, conditions, and constitutional rights. This book highlights opportunities for building a mass proletarian party able to lead the struggle to end capitalist rule, opening a socialist future for humanity. $10. Also in Spanish and French.

Malcolm X, Black Liberation, and the Road to Workers Power

JACK BARNES

The conquest of state power by a class-conscious vanguard of the working class is the mightiest weapon working people can wield against racism and Black oppression, as well as Jew-hatred and every form of human degradation inherited from class society. $20. Also in Spanish, French, Farsi, Arabic, Greek.

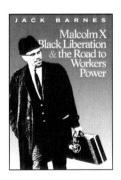

Are They Rich Because They're Smart?

Class, Privilege, and Learning under Capitalism

JACK BARNES

Exposes growing class inequalities in the US and the self-serving rationalizations of well-paid professionals who think their "brilliance" equips them to "regulate" working people, who don't know what's in our own best interest. $10. Also in Spanish, French, Farsi, Arabic.

Lenin's Final Fight

Speeches and Writings, 1922–23

V.I. LENIN

In 1922 and 1923, V.I. Lenin, central leader of the world's first socialist revolution, waged what was to be his last political battle—one that was lost after his death. At stake was whether that revolution, and the international communist movement it led, would remain on the revolutionary proletarian course that brought workers and peasants to power in October 1917. $17. Also in Spanish, Farsi, Greek.

The Transitional Program for Socialist Revolution

LEON TROTSKY

The Socialist Workers Party program, drafted by Trotsky in 1938, still guides the SWP and communists the world over. The party "uncompromisingly gives battle to all political groupings tied to the apron strings of the bourgeoisie. Its task—the abolition of capitalism's domination. Its aim—socialism. Its method—the proletarian revolution." $17. Also in Farsi.

The Third International after Lenin

LEON TROTSKY

Leon Trotsky's 1928 defense of the Marxist course that had guided the Communist International in its early years. Writing in the heat of political battle, Trotsky addresses the key challenge facing working people today: building communist parties throughout the world capable of leading workers and farmers to take power. $20. Also in Farsi.

The Teamster Series

FARRELL DOBBS

Four books on the strikes, organizing drives, and political campaigns that transformed the Teamsters across the Midwest in the 1930s into a militant industrial union movement. Written by Farrell Dobbs, the general organizer of these Teamster battles and leader of the Socialist Workers Party.

A tool for workers seeking to use union power in every workplace and advance the fight for an independent labor party. $16 each, series $50. Also in Spanish. *Teamster Rebellion* is also available in French, Farsi, Greek.

In Defense of Marxism

Against the Petty-Bourgeois Opposition in the Socialist Workers Party

LEON TROTSKY

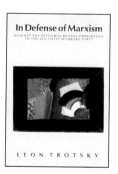

A reply to those in the revolutionary workers movement in the late 1930s buckling to bourgeois patriotism during Washington's buildup to enter World War II. Trotsky explains why only a party fighting to bring workers into its ranks and leadership can steer a communist course. In the process, he defends the materialist and dialectical foundations of Marxism. $17. Also in Spanish.

The Struggle for a Proletarian Party

JAMES P. CANNON

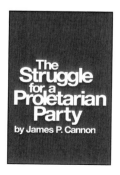

"The workers of America have power enough to topple the structure of capitalism at home and to lift the whole world with them when they rise," Cannon asserts. On the eve of World War II, a founder of the communist movement in the US and leader of the Communist International in Lenin's time defends the program and party-building norms of Bolshevism. $20. Also in Spanish and Farsi.

BUILDING A REVOLUTIONARY WORKERS PARTY

The Turn to Industry
Forging a Proletarian Party

JACK BARNES

A book about the working-class program, composition, and course of conduct of the only kind of party worthy of the name "revolutionary" in the imperialist epoch. A party that can recognize the most revolutionary fact of this epoch—the worth of working people, and our power to change society when we organize and act against the capitalist class. It's about building such a party in the US and in other capitalist countries. $15. Also in Spanish, French, Greek.

Tribunes of the People and the Trade Unions

KARL MARX, V.I. LENIN, LEON TROTSKY
FARRELL DOBBS, JACK BARNES

A tribune of the people uses every example of capitalist oppression to explain why working people, in class battles, will break from the bosses' parties, organize a revolutionary fight for state power, and lay the foundations of a socialist world of human solidarity. $12. Also in Spanish, French, Farsi, Greek.

Socialism on Trial
Testimony at Minneapolis Sedition Trial

JAMES P. CANNON

The revolutionary program of the working class, presented in response to frame-up charges of "seditious conspiracy" in 1941, on the eve of US entry into World War II. The defendants were leaders of the Minneapolis labor movement and the Socialist Workers Party. $15. Also in Spanish, French, Farsi.

Revolutionary Continuity

Marxist Leadership in the U.S.

The Early Years, 1848–1917
Birth of the Communist Movement, 1918–1922

FARRELL DOBBS

"Successive generations of proletarian revolutionists have participated in the movements of the working class and its allies. . . . Marxists today owe them not only homage for their deeds. We also have a duty to learn what they did wrong as well as right so their errors are not repeated." —*Farrell Dobbs*. Two volumes, $17 each.

The First Ten Years of American Communism

Report of a Participant

JAMES P. CANNON

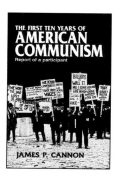

"Stalinism has worked mightily to obliterate the honorable record of American communism in its pioneer days. Yet the Communist Party wrote such a chapter too, and the young militants of the new generation ought to know about it and claim it for their own. It belongs to them." —*James P. Cannon*, 1962. $17

The Communist Manifesto

KARL MARX
AND FREDERICK ENGELS

Communism, say the founding leaders of the revolutionary workers movement, is not a set of ideas or preconceived "principles" but workers' line of march to power, springing from a "movement going on under our very eyes." $5. Also in Spanish, French, Farsi, Arabic.

The truth about the Moscow Trials

THE CASE OF LEON TROTSKY

TESTIMONY BEFORE 1937 COMMISSION INVESTIGATING CHARGES
MADE AGAINST HIM IN MOSCOW TRIALS

Was the regime of Joseph Stalin and his heirs a continuation of the Bolshevik-led workers and peasants government established by the October 1917 Revolution?

No! says Bolshevik leader Leon Trotsky in testimony before a 1937 international commission of inquiry into Stalin's Moscow frame-up trials. Reviewing forty years of working- class struggle in which Trotsky was a participant and leader, he discusses the fight to restore V.I. Lenin's revolutionary internationalist course and why the Stalin regime organized the Moscow Trials.

He explains working people's stake in the unfolding Spanish Revolution, the fight against fascism in Germany, efforts to build a world revolutionary party, and much more. $28

Companion volume **NOT GUILTY**

FINDINGS OF THE 1937 COMMISSION

"The Moscow Trials were a frame-up" said the 1937 commisision of inquiry into charges leveled against Trotsky in Stalin's kangaroo court. Full text of report. $23

My Life
Leon Trotsky

A leader of the Russian Revolution, Red Army, and the fight to maintain Lenin's continuity recounts lessons from battles he took part in from the early 1900s to his forced exile in 1929 from the Soviet Union by Stalin's counterrevolutionary regime. $27

CUBA'S SOCIALIST REVOLUTION

New Edition!
Che Guevara on Economics and Politics in the Transition to Socialism

CARLOS TABLADA

It's essential for working people to win state power, said Ernesto Che Guevara. "Then there's the second stage, maybe more difficult than the first"—the transition from dog-eat-dog capitalism to socialism. That includes moving from work as a condition for survival, to voluntary social labor through which we express our common humanity. Includes Fidel Castro's 1987 speech "Che's Ideas are Absolutely Relevant Today." New edition with substantially expanded selections from Guevara's writings. $17. Also in Spanish, coming in French.

Cuba and the Coming American Revolution

JACK BARNES

This is a book about the example set by the Cuban people that revolution is not only necessary—it can be made. A book about the struggles of workers and other exploited producers in the imperialist heartland, and the youth attracted to them. About the class struggle in the US, where the revolutionary capacities of working people are as utterly discounted by the ruling powers as were those of the Cuban toilers. And just as wrongly. $10. Also in Spanish, French, Farsi.

Women in Cuba: The Making of a Revolution within the Revolution

VILMA ESPÍN, ASELA DE LOS SANTOS, YOLANDA FERRER

The integration of women in the ranks and leadership of the Cuban Revolution was intertwined with the proletarian course of the leadership of the revolution from the start. This is the story of that revolution and how it transformed the women and men who made it. $17. Also in Spanish, Farsi, Greek.

THE WORKING CLASS AND THE FIGHT AGAINST JEW-HATRED

The Jewish Question
A Marxist Interpretation

ABRAM LEON

The battle against reactionary forces aiming to exterminate the Jews remains central to world politics, as shown by the genocidal October 2023 pogrom in Israel. Why is Jew-hatred still raising its ugly head? What are its class roots? Why, as Abram Leon explains, is there no solution "independent of the world proletarian revolution"? Revised translation, new introduction, and 40 pages of illustrations and maps. $17. Also in Spanish and French.

The Founding of the Socialist Workers Party
Minutes and Resolutions, 1938–39

JAMES P. CANNON

"The attack against Jews is a spearhead of the attack against the American working class," says an SWP resolution adopted in 1938. The party demanded that Washington "throw open the doors of the US to victims of the Hitlerite pogrom regime!" $23

Their Trotsky and Ours

JACK BARNES

To lead the working class in a successful revolution, a mass proletarian party is needed whose cadres, well beforehand, have absorbed a world communist program, are proletarian in life and work, derive deep satisfaction from doing politics, and have forged a leadership with an acute sense of what to do next. This book is about building such a party. $12. Also in Spanish, French, Farsi.

New International

A MAGAZINE OF MARXIST POLITICS AND THEORY

NEW INTERNATIONAL NO. 7

Opening Guns of World War III: Washington's Assault on Iraq

JACK BARNES

The murderous assault on Iraq in 1990–91 heralded increasingly sharp conflicts among imperialist powers, growing instability of capitalism, and more wars. Also includes:

1945: When US Troops Said No!
by Mary-Alice Waters

Lessons from the Iran-Iraq War
by Samad Sharif

$14. Also in Spanish, French, Farsi.

NEW INTERNATIONAL NO. 12

Capitalism's Long Hot Winter Has Begun

JACK BARNES

Today's global capitalist crisis is but the opening stage of decades of economic, financial, and social convulsions and class battles. Class-conscious workers confront this historic turning point for imperialism with confidence, Jack Barnes writes, drawing satisfaction from being "in their face" as we chart a revolutionary course to take power. $14. Also in Spanish, French, Farsi, Arabic, Greek.

NEW INTERNATIONAL NO. 11

U.S. Imperialism Has Lost the Cold War

JACK BARNES

The collapse of regimes across Eastern Europe and the USSR claiming to be communist did not mean workers and farmers there had been crushed. In today's sharpening class conflicts and wars, these toilers are joining working people the world over in the struggle against capitalist exploitation. $14. Also in Spanish, French, Farsi, Greek.

EXPAND YOUR REVOLUTIONARY LIBRARY

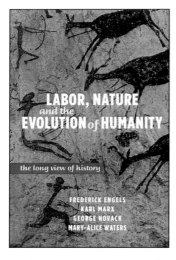

Labor, Nature, and the Evolution of Humanity

The Long View of History

FREDERICK ENGELS, KARL MARX
GEORGE NOVACK
MARY-ALICE WATERS

Without understanding that social labor, transforming nature, has driven humanity's evolution for millions of years, working people are unable to see beyond the capitalist epoch of class exploitation that warps all human relations, ideas, and values. Only the revolutionary conquest of state power by the working class can open the door to a world free of capitalist exploitation, degradation of nature, subjugation of women, racism, and war. A world built on human solidarity. A socialist world. $12. Also in Spanish and French.

Cosmetics, Fashions, and the Exploitation of Women

JOSEPH HANSEN, EVELYN REED
MARY-ALICE WATERS

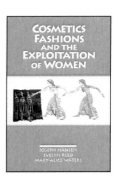

How big business reinforces women's second-class status and uses it to rake in profits. Where does women's oppression come from? How has the entry of millions of women into the workforce strengthened the battle for emancipation, still to be won? $12. Also in Spanish, Farsi, Greek.

Malcolm X Talks to Young People

"The young generation of whites, Blacks, browns, whatever else—you're living at a time of revolution," said Malcolm in 1964. "And I for one will join with anyone, I don't care what color you are, as long as you want to change this miserable condition that exists on this earth." Four talks and an interview in the last months of Malcolm's life. $12. Also in Spanish, French, Farsi, Greek.

Maurice Bishop Speaks
The Grenada Revolution and Its Overthrow, 1979–83

The triumph of the 1979 revolution in the Caribbean island of Grenada under the leadership of Maurice Bishop gave hope to millions throughout the Americas. Invaluable lessons from the workers and farmers government destroyed by a Stalinist-led counterrevolution in 1983. $20

Thomas Sankara Speaks
The Burkina Faso Revolution, 1983–87

Under Sankara's guidance, Burkina Faso's revolutionary government led peasants, workers, women, and youth to expand literacy; to sink wells, plant trees, erect housing; to combat women's oppression; to carry out land reform; to join others worldwide to free themselves from the imperialist yoke. $20. Also in French.

Pathfinder Press **accessible e-books** for the blind, those with low vision, or other challenges reading print books

For a list of current accessible titles, go to: pathfinderpress.com/collections/books-for-the-blind.

Visit bookshare.org for information on how to sign up.

HFINDER AROUND THE WORLD

UNITED STATES
(and Caribbean, Latin America, and East Asia)

Pathfinder Books, 306 W. 37th St., 13th Floor
New York, NY 10018

CANADA

Pathfinder Books, 7107 St. Denis, Suite 204
Montreal, QC H2S 2S5

UNITED KINGDOM
(and Europe, Africa, Middle East, and South Asia)

Pathfinder Books, 5 Norman Rd.
Seven Sisters, London N15 4ND

AUSTRALIA
(and New Zealand, Southeast Asia, and the Pacific)

Pathfinder Books, Suite 2, First floor, 275 George St.
Liverpool, Sydney, NSW 2170
Postal address: P.O. Box 73, Campsie, NSW 2194

JOIN THE PATHFINDER READERS CLUB
BUILD YOUR LIBRARY!

$10 / YEAR
25% DISCOUNT ON ALL PATHFINDER TITLES
30% OFF BOOKS OF THE MONTH
Valid at pathfinderpress.com and local Pathfinder book centers

Go to: pathfinderpress.com/
products/pathfinder-readers-club

Pathfinder
pathfinderpress.com